The Joy of Patterns

Using Patterns for Enterprise Development

The Software Patterns Series

Series Editor: John M. Vlissides

The Software Patterns Series (SPS) comprises pattern literature of lasting significance to software developers. Software patterns document general solutions to recurring problems in all software-related spheres, from the technology itself, to the organizations that develop and distribute it, to the people who use it. Books in the series distill experience from one or more of these areas into a form that software professionals can apply immediately. *Relevance* and *impact* are the tenets of the SPS. Relevance means each book presents patterns that solve real problems. Patterns worthy of the name are intrinsically relevant; they are borne of practitioners' experiences, not theory or speculation. Patterns have impact when they change how people work for the better. A book becomes a part of the series not just because it embraces these tenets, but because it has demonstrated it fulfills them for its audience.

Titles in the series:

The Design Patterns Smalltalk Companion, Sherman Alpert/Kyle Brown/Bobby Woolf

The Joy of Patterns: Using Patterns for Enterprise Development, Brandon Goldfedder

The Manager Pool: Patterns for Radical Leadership, Don Olson/Carol Stimmel

The Pattern Almanac 2000, Linda Rising

Pattern Hatching: Design Patterns Applied, John Vlissides

Pattern Languages of Program Design, edited by James O. Coplien/Douglas C. Schmidt

Pattern Languages of Program Design 2, edited by John M. Vlissides/James O. Coplien/
    Norman L. Kerth

Pattern Languages of Program Design 3, edited by Robert Martin/Dirk Riehle/
    Frank Buschmann

Pattern Languages of Program Design 4, edited by Neil Harrison/Brian Foote/
    Hans Rohnert

Small Memory Software, James Noble/Charles Weir

Please see our web site at http://www.awl.com/cseng/swpatterns
for more information on these titles.

THE JOY OF PATTERNS

Using Patterns for Enterprise Development

Brandon Goldfedder

✦✦ Addison-Wesley

Boston • San Francisco • New York • Toronto • Montreal
London • Munich • Paris • Madrid
Capetown • Sydney • Tokyo • Singapore • Mexico City

The publisher offers discounts on this book when ordered in quantity for special sales. For more information, please contact:

Pearson Education Corporate Sales Division
201 W. 103rd Street
Indianapolis, IN 46290
(800) 428-5531
corpsales@pearsoned.com

Visit AW on the Web: www.aw.com/cseng/

Library of Congress Cataloging-in-Publication Data

Goldfedder, Brandon
   The joy of patterns : using patterns for enterprise development /Brandon Goldfedder
      p. cm. -- (The software patterns series)
   Includes bibliographical references and index.
   ISBN 0-201-65759-7 (alk. paper)
      1. Computer software--Development. I. Title. II. Series.

   QA76.76.D47 G64 2001
   005.1--dc21   2001041300

For information on obtaining permission for use of material from this work, please submit a written request to:

Pearson Education, Inc.
Rights and Contracts Department
75 Arlington Street, Suite 300
Boston, MA 02116
Fax: (617) 848-7047

ISBN: 0-201-65759-7
Text printed on recycled paper
1 2 3 4 5 6 7 8 9 10—CRS—0504030201
First printing, September 2001

To Susan, who forms the context of my world.

Contents

Preface   *xi*

Acknowledgments   *xiii*

CHAPTER 1   *Initial Thoughts: A Personal Note*   *1*

Background   1
Summary   5

CHAPTER 2   *An Introduction to Patterns*   *7*

The Building Blocks of Architecture   7
Pattern Form   9
    Patterns: The Language of Design   17
    Documentation   22
    Extensible Software Development and Change Management   23
    Training   27
    Silver Bullets   28
Summary   28

CHAPTER 3   *OO at a Glance*   *31*

Introduction   31
    Inheritance   34
    Components   41
Summary   42

CHAPTER 4   *A Product Configurator   45*

Introduction   45

Problem Definition   45

Solution   47
   Observations   48
   Composite   49

Sample   59

CHAPTER 5   *BurgerShop 101   61*

Overview   61

Sue's Burger Shop   61
   Reflections   72
   Simplifications   73

Summary   75

CHAPTER 6   *Programming Languages and Patterns   77*

   Java Observer   82

Summary   84

CHAPTER 7   *Patterns and System Development   85*

Building from Scratch   85
   Understanding Your Requirements   86
   Create Hinge Points for the Unknowns and Entities that We
      Suspect Are Likely to Change   87
   Utilize Supporting Patterns to Ensure No Loose Ends   91
   Make a Sanity Check   92
   Implement a Little   92
   Restart the Whole Process at a Lower Level, as Necessary   95

Summary   96

CHAPTER 8   *Patterns and System Evolution (Maintenance)   97*

Maintenance   97

A Quick Example   101

Summary   106

CHAPTER 9   *Closing Thoughts*   109

APPENDIX A   *Product Code*   111

APPENDIX B   *BurgerShop Code*   125

APPENDIX C   *Blackjack Code*   143

References   167

Index   171

Preface

What's it all about?

This book is about the practice of correctly applying patterns to build software systems. It is intended to complement the outstanding body of patterns available by educating the reader on the general concepts of proper use that hold true regardless of the specific pattern or system. Far too often developers and managers who first attempt to use patterns fail to do so properly because they completely miss the intent and simple concepts involved; instead, they tend to focus on patterns as coding tricks rather than as a higher-level language for describing system design. This book attempts to fix this problem by providing the reader the tools necessary to ensure success.

In the first basic software design course I ever taught, we struggled over how someone could actually "teach" design. What we determined to be the best approach was to present the trade-offs and heuristics through the use of examples and to allow the participants to learn in this manner. I still believe this is a fundamental way to teach design and have tried to carry it forward in my training classes, in my consulting, and also in this book.

The approach I have taken in this book is to provide this insight through a series of system designs from initial conception through code. I recognized early in instructing this type of material that, while design has little to do with code, it is still essential to show the resulting programming language code that is the real end product of system development. I provide many examples to illustrate the use of patterns to build systems that will be implemented in one of three currently popular programming languages: Visual Basic, C++, and Java. While I do dive into the depth of the code to illustrate key points, I have tried not to require a lot of programming or other formal training for the reader.

In order to focus on using patterns rather than on trying to survey the depth of patterns now available,[1] I primarily focus on a core subset of patterns in this book, primarily those originally captured in the now classic *Design Patterns* [Gam, 95]. I will augment this essential set with a few unique patterns of my own and of other authors where appropriate.

This book is intended to be read in the order it is presented, although readers may feel free to skip around as they need to. However, I would still suggest reading Chapter 2, "An Introduction to Patterns" before reading other sections. The general approach used in this book is first to introduce the readers to patterns and a subset of object-oriented concepts and notations so that we are all on the same page. I then quickly move into the examples to show the application of patterns to address different problems and show the pros and cons that result as guiding decisions in the system architecture are made.

When I teach patterns, there is usually a point at the beginning of the courses when people simply do not get the mental shift required to look at software development in a new manner. As an instructor I can tell by the glazed look in the students' eyes (although that is often due to the morning caffeine not yet setting in). Suddenly about a third of the way through the material, students start to pull the pieces together and realize that patterns are simply more than coding tricks or language techniques. This paradigm shift seems suddenly to come to the students, and they quickly grasp the importance of these techniques on their entire approach to software development.

My hope is that you, the reader of this material, will think about the material and the examples and gain this same enlightenment. This will occur quickly once we can recognize that there are inherent forces at work in software design, and we can approach the problem from a more esthetic nature, rather than simply as a coding technique. You will begin to look at patterns as a key tool in design and be able to use patterns properly; equally important, you will know how and when not to use them. The ability to look at a problem in terms of the forces at work and the context will greatly improve all subsequent efforts. At this point our goals will have succeeded.

I hope you enjoy the journey.

---

1. For readers wishing to gather a larger catalog of patterns, I highly recommend Linda Rising's, *The Patterns Almanac* [Ris, 00] as a reference source.

Acknowledgments

Thanks to my reviewers and their feedback, including Jeff Aikin, Steve Berczuk, Bob Hanmer, Neil Harrison, and Linda Rising. Thanks to Paul Becker, my editor, for his continual advice and directions as this project went on far longer than I would have believed. Thanks also to Jacquelyn Doucette, my production manager, and Bunny Ames, my copyeditor, for "Englishifying" this work and making it far more readable.

And most important, special thanks to my best friend, Susan, to whom I am lucky enough to be married, who spent many late nights reviewing my notes, fixing my spelling, and keeping me semisane as I completed this work.

Chapter

1

Initial Thoughts: A Personal Note

Background

I started programming at the age of twelve thanks to a close friend of the family who gave me a certificate for a Radio Shack computer course. I was lucky that the local store liked the idea of having a twelve-year-old programming their computers because it showed how truly easy computers were to use. Since that time, I have spent every day (except for a handful of vacation days when I was forbidden to bring a computer with me) programming or otherwise developing software at some level. I think this explains the warped view of the world I am so often credited with.

Now, more than twenty years and many hundreds of thousands of lines of code later, I get a chance to share a piece of what I find important. I have been amazingly lucky to learn from plenty of smart people, both colleagues on projects and students in various training courses I have taught. During this process I have learned lots of techniques and approaches—some of them helpful; some I had to unlearn. Certain key techniques, once internalized, changed my view on software development as a whole.

In 1994, I was working on an embedded pen-based system that was intended as a specialized notebook-size form entry device (much like a larger-size Palm Pilot). This was one of those many technical projects that met its objectives but never really achieved the market space it needed for commercial success. At that time I started to notice several idioms or common techniques that I had used and that had been used in other systems, both at my current company and at other companies I had worked for. We spent a while trying to come up with ways to document and refine the techniques.

It was at this point that a friend directed me to the patterns work being compiled, and I delved into this area, exploring the work done by Christopher Alexander and others. I discovered that not only did these patterns address the same type of things we were doing, but they opened my eyes to a whole new way of looking at problems and understanding system architecture as a whole. I also discovered many things I had done wrong in the past and finally understood why some of our previous efforts had failed. I resolved not to repeat those errors and to come up with ways to share this knowledge with others.

Let's jump right in. Let me show you one of the first patterns I wrote and one that forms one of the key tenets I try to use when designing any software system. I'll present it here quickly. Later, I'll explain the key sections of the pattern and show its application throughout the book. However, I think it is important to understand that whether you agree with it, a pattern forms a picture in your mind, conveying the key concepts and application in a readily accessible manner.

⚎ ⚎ ⚎ ⚎

Pattern Name: High Road Development[1]

Problem

How do you handle existing requirements efficiently in the face of changing and future requirements?

Context

Developers build or extend a system.

Forces

- Future requirements are often not fully understood and are highly subject to change.

---

1. Steve Berczuk suggested the great alternative name, High Road Development, pointing out that noun phrases for patterns are normally far superior than my earlier verb-phase name, Build for Today, Design for Tomorrow

- Efforts in reuse often lead to elaborate components that are not reusable and often fail to be completed.
- It is often unclear and easy to lose sight of what is a "future" vs. current requirement.
- Developers tend to look at any problem only as a coding problem; they fail to consider the power of design to solve these types of problems.
- C++ and other object-oriented languages provide ways in which to build flexibility through mechanisms such as virtual methods and templates. Unfortunately, many developers do not properly utilize these tools.

Solution

Never write any unneeded code in the implementation; instead, transfer the effort to design. Ensure that the architecture can handle all potential scenarios (realistically, as many likely ones as possible). This is a rather lofty goal, but movement in this direction is essential. Rather than hardcode in code that is rigid, utilize design patterns and other mechanisms to allow the system to expand through additional variations rather than through change. In addition, avoid the use of any stub code or other placeholder where an additional level of indirection and application of a pattern can allow the solution to be more readily solved.

Resulting Context

What results is a system that meets existing requirements and is capable of addressing future requirements when necessary. The cost of adding these new capabilities is often less than if an up-front effort had been made. This is especially true when we don't know up front the exact requirements (otherwise we might have done it initially), so our up-front efforts are often wrong or result in development toward a less optimal design. One area to watch carefully when applying this pattern is the resulting potential increase in design complexity (although not always coding complexity).

Rationale

By shifting the focus from implementation to design, we can solve higher-level problems more effectively and often dismiss the problem entirely. Often the features that the system is supposed to handle are never implemented, and other features come into existence because of market forces. Normally these new features can be easily handled since the architecture has been made extensible.

Aliases

Build for Today, Design for Tomorrow

Known Uses

This pattern has been applied to several large frameworks that I developed. One example is Total Commissions Systems (TCS), an enterprise-level commission calculation system. In this specific system, the application of this pattern allowed us rapidly to redesign the core calculation portions between Versions 1 and 2 to decouple the hardcoding to a plug-in architecture. This change took a matter of days and avoided significant ripple throughout the system.

▨ ▨ ▨ ▨

SIDEBAR: Refactoring and Extreme Programming

Refactoring [Fow, 99] provides an alternative approach to using this pattern, and, if a sufficient testing framework exists, it can be utilized successfully. A fundamental idea in refactoring is to focus on simplifying design and to provide an environment for continual evolution (rather than extension) as new requirements emerge. When an approach that is based on refactoring is used, a development approach, such as *Extreme Programming Explained: Embrace (XP)* [Bec, 00], should be considered.

From a very high level, XP is a team-based approach in which the division between the different cycles blurs because of an extremely reduced time frame for each phase. This approach is just beginning to gain some attention (although similar processes including RAD and Just In Time programming have been used successfully for many years). XP seems to work well for in-house projects in environments of high risk and change where standard processes may fail. I think it also works best with teams consisting of more junior programmers.

This is a very controversial approach, and I'm still at the investigation stage of this process. I have found much with which I disagree, mainly because of environmental issues in the type of development I've observed, but I enjoy anything that makes me question what I thought I knew. I highly recommend learning about this approach. Beck's book [Bec, 00] is an extremely quick read and raises several questions about the process of developing software. Regardless of the process or specific approach used, the approaches discussed in this book should be fundamentally considered when building any software systems.

Summary

Throughout this book and in systems that I helped to develop, I attempt to apply this technique as a predominating principle in building systems. This eliminates my designs and limits the ability to extend a system as new requirements come in. This further provides a guideline for applying other patterns. Throughout this book, I will explore ways in which to ensure that you can gain the same flexibility and power of design.

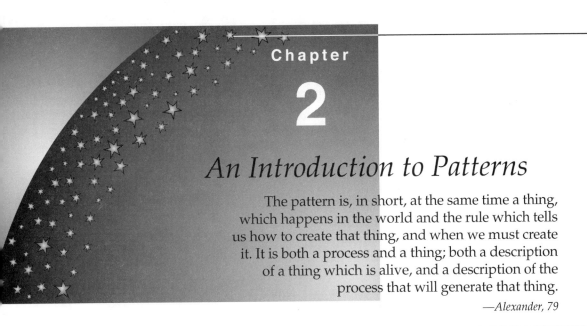

An Introduction to Patterns

The pattern is, in short, at the same time a thing,
which happens in the world and the rule which tells
us how to create that thing, and when we must create
it. It is both a process and a thing; both a description
of a thing which is alive, and a description of the
process that will generate that thing.

—*Alexander, 79*

The Building Blocks of Architecture

Software is less like a snowflake, where every one is truly unique, and more like a LEGO set. We can combine the Legos in many configurations to make whatever shapes we need at the time, but the key building blocks are the same. However, these building blocks are more than simple algorithms and data structures; patterns are more than these building blocks or Legos themselves. They are closer to the molds that form the different Legos. They provide a way to ensure that any Legos made from the mold will work with each other, providing additional support and definition as more Legos are connected.

More specifically, the different parts of a software architecture solve problems that are not unique. The same problems keep surfacing in many different systems, regardless of the type of customer domain. Let's look at a specific example. Often in software we need to handle multiple objects that are dependent on the state of another object. For example, in an accounting system you may provide multiple views of the data, perhaps multiple spreadsheet views as well as graphical views. Whenever you change the data in one spreadsheet, the user would reasonably expect the other views to change (automatically, without selecting a refresh option).

Patterns, though, transcend a specific domain. For example, in an embedded system you may have a similar problem of multiple objects (such as monitors) watching a piece of hardware (through its software encapsulation/device

7

driver) that has to react quickly when an interrupt such as low power occurs. A pattern can describe this situation and address how to proceed in a readily transferable manner. For example, this monitoring approach is described as the Observer Pattern [Gam, 95], summarized here:

Observer Pattern

Intent

Define a one-to-many dependency between objects so that when one object changes state, all of its dependents are notified and updated automatically.

Varies

Varies the number of objects that depend on one another and how the dependent objects stay up-to-date.

Structure

Figure 2.1 illustrates the Observer Pattern structure.

Comments

The Observer Pattern is also referred to as publisher-subscriber [Bus, 96] and is a major aspect in the document-view concept. The complexity in the

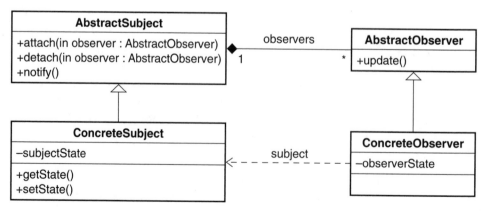

Figure 2.1   *Observer Pattern Structure*

Observer Pattern is often an implementation decision such as whether to use a push model (and send the data about the subject to the observer) or to use a pull model (and have the observer obtain the information it needs). Often a proxy pattern [Gam, 95] is used with the observer to allow remote observers to be used. If some of the clients are remote, you need to consider whether to use push or pull notification because of the perfomance implications of remote notifications and network overhead issues.

⊠ ⊠ ⊠ ⊠

Pattern Form

One of the key goals of patterns is to capture the solutions to these reoccurring problems (and the constraints or context in which they can be used) in a manner which is easily accessible to others.

When we capture this information, we attempt to understand the underlying reasons about why this solution works. At this point, we can often generalize and gain a deeper understanding of the different aspects at work. In doing this "harvesting" of information, we often uncover related patterns that may also provide equal or greater value. In addition, by looking explicitly at the forces and other elements of the problem, we gain an amazing insight into the nature of software development.

Perhaps most pragmatically, and unlike traditional documentation approaches, patterns can be used to document systems at a higher level of abstraction, allowing dynamic, as well as static, behavior to be captured. The value of this form of documentation for knowledge transfer cannot be overstated.

A pattern can be written in one of several forms. While the exact form does not matter, keeping to some form takes one more thing off the pattern writer's mind and allows the writer to address the true problems. Regardless of the form used, every form should contain, in some manner, the following:

Name/Aliases: A pattern must be uniquely named so it can be internalized in the reader's mind. A name must be memorable and must evolve the system. A pattern, though, may have several names by which it is known. This sometimes creates confusion.

Problem: The form should include the specific problem that the pattern addresses. If we consider that the problem portion is a somewhat abstract statement of what we are trying to accomplish, then the solution is the mechanism we can use to accomplish our goal. Because a problem may have many solutions, how do we determine the best or the "correct" solution? Well, first we must add another piece to this equation—forces.

Forces: Forces are any considerations that must be taken into account. These are the things that make the problem hard and make the obvious solutions invalid. We can think of forces as considerations that the pattern must reconcile. There are an infinite number of forces present, so we must prioritize these forces into a context. Forces include environmental issues, language issues, organization issues, and platform issues. For example, a Telecom UNIX development effort using Java in a highly skilled development team may bring to bear different forces than a financial mainframe development effort using COBOL. When a pattern is selected, it resolves many of the forces but leaves with both strong and weak forces that remain to be resolved by other patterns.

A good pattern choice should resolve the forces still to be addressed. The pattern carves and builds on other patterns in the system to make them stronger. Much like the jigsaw puzzle in Figure 2.2, as more pieces are added, the puzzle as a whole becomes more stable. In addition, if the wrong piece is forced into the puzzle, it becomes more likely to spring up and break. Think of the puzzle as the system and the pieces as the patterns, and you can start to see system dynamics in new ways.

However, recognizing the forces at work can be extremely complex. One place where similar forces exist is in chess (see Figure 2.3). If we consider chess from one strategic view, it really is about reinforcing certain forces to cancel out other forces. The goal, of course, is to supply sufficient force to the opposing king and to areas around the king to guarantee that your opponent is overwhelmed.

When patterns are combined appropriately, they should form a complex system that is in harmony. Each pattern should reinforce the others, mak-

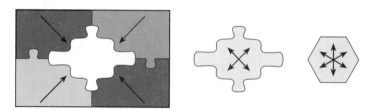

Figure 2.2   *Forces apply pressure and reinforce the whole like jigsaw puzzle pieces*

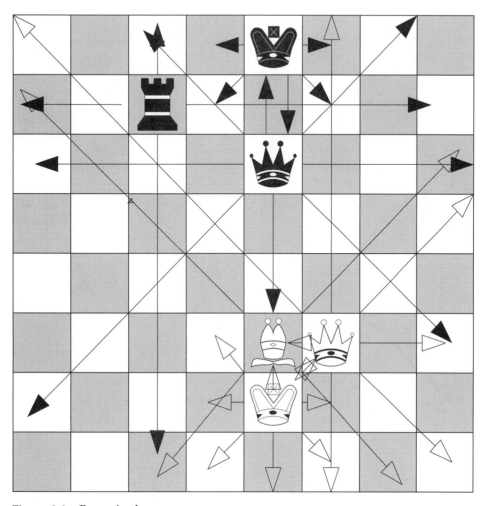

Figure 2.3 *Forces in chess*

Source: Visio Template by Dennis K. Fitzgerald, CIS 72627, 1442 template found on Web/Visio Group.

ing the system stronger with each addition. In this manner a system may continue to evolve without hitting the maintenance burden or breakdown effect that often results as the system continues to be enhanced. What we are hoping to do is to create a reinforcing framework (see Figure 2.4) where each added piece makes all of the other parts stronger.

A pattern does not exist in a vacuum. In fact, a pattern depends not only on the specific pattern itself but also on every other pattern that is part of the total architecture. Each pattern composes itself of other pieces and creates dependents. In the same way that a small number of words leads to

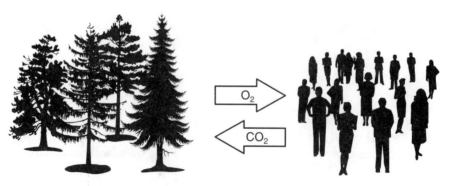

Figure 2.4   *A reinforcing framework*

the expression of many complex ideas, a small number of patterns can yield many complex systems. The proper application of patterns should create a system that is in order and complete but still extensible. In all cases, a system of harmony should exist.

As you get more comfortable with patterns, you can start to look at any problem you are trying to solve as a diagram of forces and understand that anything you put in will have an impact. Hopefully, that impact will be to harmonize the forces you want to resolve.

Unfortunately in software, developers often approach a problem without really thinking about the forces at work or understanding the real problems at play. This results in a novice developer jumping into coding without really knowing how, or even if, a coding solution is appropriate. Taking a step back to understand what is really at work and then choosing the appropriate tools can save many thousands of lines of code and much wasted effort.

Often the real problems and forces are the unknowns, but we still have to develop our systems in spite of this. This is where the use of patterns is all the more essential. The unknowns become strong forces to which we must apply a pattern in order to resolve and reduce the risk of getting it wrong. By understanding the areas that are unknown, we can apply a pattern to provide for the variance when we finally understand the problem—this becomes the real challenge of design. If all the requirements were known up front and were unlikely to change, then design would be a trivial exercise. Luckily, few of us live in a world that is boring; instead we are faced with the constant challenge of change.

Context: Context includes any and all constraints on the solution usually formed by the application of other patterns to the system. Context serves to help prioritize strong and weak forces. Each pattern applied to a system further constrains subsequent patterns.

Solutions: The solution to the problem is within this context.

Motivation/Examples/Known Uses: It is important to have examples that the reader can understand and internalize. The key is for readers to internalize the pattern so they don't actively have to look things up to recall them. I recall Kent Beck clearly explaining at the first Pattern Language of Programming Conference I went to that the best (and only) way to learn is through stories. That is why examples or motivation is such a clearly essential part of the pattern. People will easily remember the pattern if they can associate a story with it.

Force Resolution: Force resolution includes the forces that are resolved by this pattern and those that are not. Any special handling should also be noted.

Resulting Context/Consequences: This form element includes what is left that still needs to be resolved after applying the solution.

Design Rationale: Design rationale is why this pattern works.

In the pattern snippets that I use from the Design Patterns book [Gam, 95], I add the relevant sections from their form. These include the following:

Varies: Varies indicates for what aspect of the system these patterns provide a hinge point. All GOF patterns support some level of variation.

Structure: This is a UML-based diagram of an example software structure diagram. These drawings, while useful, often fail to address adequately the dynamic nature of the pattern.

So let's consider two examples of the base form.

First, let's look at a common pattern used to describe memory reclamation. It was written to support the documentation of an approach we were using to develop a system at a company I was working for.

Pattern Name: Recycle Bin

Problem

How do you reduce the overhead of creation and destruction of resources?

Context

A number of resources are requested and released while the system is running.

Forces

- Resource allocation, if left to the OS, may be expensive.
- Resource allocation, if left to the OS, may be shared with others.
- Resource allocation, if left to the OS, may cause fragmentation of the resource pool.
- Dynamic allocation of resources may be unsafe or unavailable on some systems.
- Small resource requests may have high overhead.

Solution

You can store freed resources in a local bin so that subsequent requests for these resources can reuse the ones in the bin. A client requests resources through the bin. The bin will reuse an existing bin, if available, or create a new one, if necessary. The recycle bin may request more resources than are actually needed to optimize performance. When the use of the resource is complete, it should be returned to the bin. A bridge (Gam, 96) may be introduced to separate the client's view of the resource from the actual resources so that the concept of the recycling bin can be completely hidden from the client. A recycle bin may create a fixed amount of resources up front or may request them on demand.

Resulting Context

We now have a system where resource allocation and deallocation may be controlled to whatever level the situation calls for.

Rationale

Resource requests normally go through the operating system. Kernel requests for resources are among the most expensive calls that can be made. Specifically, memory requests in a UNIX system can cause havoc on real-time system performance. In addition, users often misunderstand the overhead related to managing dynamic memory allocation. For example, a malloc of 2 bytes may carry an overhead that is at least 2 pointers in memory. The overhead cost is then more than the actual storage cost. Additionally, many operating systems use a minimum-size block so even more is wasted. By utilizing a recycle bin and managing the resources ourselves, no OS calls are required by the client, thus increasing our portability. All requests are essentially pointer assignments and calculations. Any additional overhead is completely controlled by the recycle bin, which can then take advantage of low-level optimizations without sacrificing portability of the clients.

Known Uses

This pattern has been used successfully for memory management in many systems that support the allocation of memory in large chunks. A similar approach is used in Sun's Hotspot Java environment through the use of nurseries.

Related Patterns

Bridge [Gam, 95]

Sketch

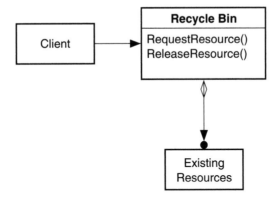

Author(s)

Brandon Goldfedder

Date(s)

9/25/95

Patterns don't have to be about writing software at all. Consider the following somewhat tongue-in-cheek pattern.

▨ ▨ ▨ ▨

Pattern Name: Scream Test

Problem

How do you determine if an aspect of the system is in use?

Context

A system has a feature that is advantageous to phase out. This pattern also applies to networks in which it is unknown if active users are using a program. In all cases, a functional equivalence of the program should exist.

Forces

- It is often difficult to tell if users are using a program or a feature or if its importance to the users after an alternative is available.
- If you ask users, you will often get resistance to change.
- Louder users may be more important than quieter ones; then again, they may not. . . .
- The careless application of this pattern may reflect poorly on the implementer. This fear may keep it from being properly applied.
- A help desk or other avenue for users to complain must exist.

Solution

Temporarily disable the feature (move the files, remove menu options, and so on), and place it into a hidden holding area. After a predetermined time, if no "significant" complaints are presented, the feature may be removed.

Resulting Context

Either a feature (program or option) is removed if unused, or its importance is better understood.

Rationale

If there are options available, users will often use the "better" alternative than do without. This encourages the users' exposure to the alternatives. If there are no options available, this pattern will cause this problem to surface as well.

Known Uses

Help desks and system shops everywhere.

Author(s)

Brandon Goldfedder

※ ※ ※ ※

Patterns: The Language of Design

In developing software systems, we are starting to see the possibility of an evolution in the way in which we communicate. Program languages and our way of describing them began with machine code, a series of binary values (1s and 0s) to represent electronic switch placements. Each unique switch alignment could represent a command or a value represented by the machine. Common combinations of legal arrangements gained mnemonic meanings. For example, 0101 0001 might mean load the accumulator with the value 1. Assembly-level languages evolved to allow this to be specified as LDA 0x1. This more efficient mechanism allowed for increased productivity in communicating with the machine. Higher-level languages, such as FORTRAN and COBOL, continued to evolve, allowing domain-specific concepts[1] to be expressed by providing a syntax and semantics for expressing these higher concepts.

This programming language evolution continued to evolve, allowing even more abstract concepts to be expressed. For example, structural programming languages (with the concept of modules) were replaced by languages that support object-based (such as Ada 83) and object-oriented (such as Smalltalk, C++, and Java) techniques. This language evolution was combined with common library reuse (such as those provided by the FORTRAN math library,

---

1. FORTRAN's domain is primarily for scientific and engineering approaches. COBOL's domain is primarily for business.

C++ Standard Library, and Java's many common libraries). Unfortunately, for reasons to be explained shortly, language issues became a common area of disagreement and division among many IT professionals.

Recall, though, that the concepts we are describing, albeit at higher levels, are still what we want to communicate to the machine. No matter what we believe, we are describing an implementation that we want the machine to perform. Unfortunately, while we have greatly improved our ability to communicate to the machine, we have not improved our ability to communicate to other developers. Implementation languages are written for machines, not for other human beings.

What is needed is to describe high-level concepts in a way in which humans can communicate design efficiently. A system and a way in which to describe larger concepts could evolve by providing such a language. As a side effect, such a language would allow us to utilize our implementation languages, which our computer needs, much more efficiently.

To summarize, we need a language to allow us to communicate and discuss common recurring design concepts efficiently and to build upon these concepts. We are looking at a way to shift from the semantics that a machine requires to the content that we use to communicate among developers. Patterns provide the words of this new, common language (Figure 2.5). Don't think about patterns merely as the solution but rather as the words that can be combined by rules to form sentences (system designs). It is important as you continue to learn about patterns to keep this idea in mind.

Consider the following scene, as illustrated in Figure 2.6: You sit in a design review meeting, and a majority of the meeting is taken up by several developers arguing about a specific function and whether a pointer or a reference should be used for passing parameters in C++ (if you don't use C++, insert

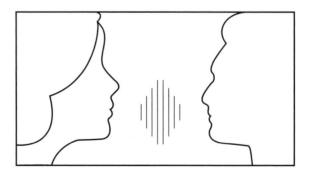

Figure 2.5   *Finding a common language*

Figure 2.6 *A "design" discussion?*

your own programming language nuance here). This discussion continues to dominate the meeting and will probably arise again in future meetings.

No doubt these types of discussions are useful, but is a design review meeting the proper place? I would not think so. Moreover, these types of conversations should be the exception rather than the rule in this type of review. That's not to say that these conversations don't have a place; they do. They should occur during a code review. It is essential to keep design reviews and code reviews separate. The real problem surfaces when these coding discussions displace the design talks that are necessary for a project's success.

If you consider the process of software development (discussed later in this chapter), it is clear that the actual implementation itself does not dominate the process. Why then is the specific programming language used? Well, it is partially because any programming language brings certain idioms (or language-specific patterns/techniques) to the table. Novice developers often do not understand the distinction between design and implementation, so these idioms are the only way they have to express design.

Why then do these things happen? To quote Maslov: "If the only tool you have is a hammer, you tend to treat everything as if it were a nail." Most developers and architects began as coders and think in terms of the tool they are most familiar with, that is, the text editor for programming code. Design is primarily a communication activity. The problem is that developers are often extremely bad communicators; their interpersonal skills often play second fiddle to their coding capability. Often a developer who cannot communicate may serve to do far more harm than good on a project.

One observation that seems to recur whenever I come to a new project is that no matter how much experience the individual developers have when they come to the project, it often seems that they are starting from scratch. The discussions on technique, languages, notation, CM tools, and so on seem to occupy far more time than is justified at this point. The initial phase of the project resembles two modems trying to find a common protocol. This is actually part of any normal communication process where each party tries to identify a common language and frame of reference.

When developers have previously worked on a project together the situation changes to that shown in Figure 2.7.

This transition is very helpful because we now have a way to discuss a higher-level concept in terms that the developers can relate to. The problems with this concept are

1. the developers may not remember things the same way;

Figure 2.7 *An established team at work*

2. this does nothing to help developers who were not part of the same project; and

3. there is no way to determine if it is necessarily the right thing to apply (see the earlier discussion about problems/solutions without a context).

SOAPBOX

Knowledge about existing systems is a double-edged sword. It can greatly benefit a project having people who have "been there; done that," but often the domain or environment of the previous projects doesn't apply anymore. Unfortunately, these experienced developers may be blinded to this. One project I worked with at a telecommunication shop attempted to build a new switch scheduling system in the same manner as its previous switches. What the developers failed to consider was that the older systems had a custom-built operating system to guarantee real-time behavior. The new switch was based on a commercial UNIX system with a commercial database where context switching was unpredictable. Needless to say, this project was less than a 100 percent success (in spite of faster hardware, new advances, and so on). If the context had been considered more carefully, the results might have been better.

Once the team has started to understand and use patterns, the conversation can change to something like that in Figure 2.8.

At this point, the vocabulary of the developers can emerge to take advantage of this newfound way to look at the systems. As the developers become more acclimated to speaking and thinking in terms of higher-level concepts, their ability to communicate abstract concepts and build better systems improves.

I often begin any new project with a few standard things in place:

1. A set of coding guidelines, valid tools, notational rules, and so on

2. An introduction to patterns course (often given in one really long day) to ensure that everyone on the team understands patterns and that they have the same understanding of terms

3. Follow-up on design reviews and additional training to ensure proper application

I have found that these standards tend to reduce drastically the time required to build highly functional development teams. This team-based approach to training has been demonstrated time and again to pay for itself many times over [Gol, 96].

Figure 2.8   *A pattern-literate team at work*

I believe that the improvement in design communication skills is one of the paramount advantages to using patterns. The ability to discuss these high-level concepts and to analyze the trade-off in design alternatives is an invaluable one for building robust extensible systems.

Documentation

One of the most troublesome activities in system development is creating good, meaningful documentation. Part of this problem (aside from the pure complexity of the systems themselves) stems from the vocabulary we use to discuss system design; part of it is historical. Most documentation techniques arise from large-scale projects that evolved from governmental standards, such as the infamous 2167.[2] These forms of documentation can do a relatively

---

2. 2167 is one of the earlier government standards of how to rigorously document a system. It was superceded by 2167A, Mil-Std-SDD, and other standards.

good job describing the components of the system itself. However, they tend to lend themselves to structured design principles. They do very little to describe the state/data of components. In addition, they fail to describe the interactions between objects. In describing complex systems and frameworks, I have found no other effective manner in which to convey the system design so that others may quickly understand and extend them.

To summarize this concept with a quote from Taligent [Tal, 94]:

> By describing the design of a framework in terms of patterns, you describe both the design and the rationale behind the design.

As a example, consider the following two options to describe how to find a number in a sorted list of values:[3]

1. Divide the list in half. Compare the value we are looking for to the middle element. If it is equal, then we have found it. If it is less than the middle value, set the new top position equal to the middle position (dividing it in half again). If it is more than the middle value, set the new bottom position equal to the middle position. Continue this division until the list cannot be divided any further. At this point if it isn't in the last two positions, it is not in the list.
2. Use binary search.

Note that the second value is more precise and easier to understand, and it is valid to use in documentation, if the following assumptions are made:

- Readers know what binary search is.
- Readers can find an implementation in a reuse library, an algorithms textbook, or their own memory.

Extensible Software Development and Change Management

One of the major failings with many development methodologies is that they fail to consider the impact of requirement changes that will occur as the product evolves. For example, several notable OO methods work great in the classroom where requirements are known up front and can never change, but they fail miserably in the real world of changing user needs.

---

3. Algorithms are not patterns, but I find this a great analogy to describe their benefits in a simple way.

One of the key goals in development is Meyers's Open-Closed Principle [Mey, 88]. This principle states that a system remain open for extension but closed for use. Simply put, "If it ain't broke, don't fix it!"

To extend a system with new functionality, you will want to write the new functionality and modify exactly one part of the existing system, the part where you decide to use this new functionality. By moving in this direction, a single point of maintenance is achieved. I like to think about this simply as being able to plug in new implementations and to extend a system much in the way that additional electronic devices can be plugged into an extension cord.

I find this way of viewing a system to be so important that I focus on it in detail throughout this book. Patterns allow us to take advantage of this principle to create large, robust systems and frameworks.

Following is a pseudocode fragment that does not subscribe to the Open-Closed Principle:

```
LegoSystem::processColor()
{
switch(color)
    {
    case RED:
            redprocess();
            break;
    case GREEN:
            greenprocess();
            break;
    case YELLOW:
            yellowprocess();
            break;
    }
}
```

Adding a new color such as orange obviously causes the code that handles green, red, and yellow to be modified. This could be resolved by the use of a State pattern [Gam, 95] that reifies (or turns into an object) this concept of color.

⊠ ⊠ ⊠ ⊠

State Pattern

Intent

Allow an object to alter its behavior when its internal state changes. The object will appear to change its class.

Varies

The internal state of an object varies.

Structure

Figure 2.9 illustrates a State structure

Comments

Use a State pattern to handle an enumerated list anywhere you see two or more similar case structures in a system. While enumerated lists make excellent candidates for the State pattern, consider carefully if it makes sense in boolean cases.

One other common consideration is whether to have the state created within the object or to use a complementary pattern such as a flyweight pattern [Gam, 95]. (A flyweight is used to pool object state, allowing a very lightweight manner to handle many objects. At the other extreme is the singleton, which avoids multiple copies of an object being created by sharing a single instance [Gam, 95].)

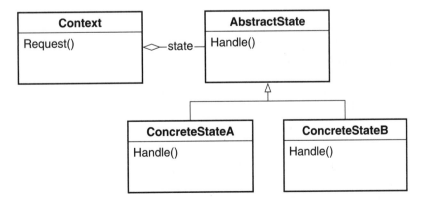

Figure 2.9   *State structure*

The nominal case is where the context selects the state. However, the State pattern can also be used where the next state to utilize is decided by the existing case. I have used this mechanism to allow rule-processing trees of system state for call processing to be loaded dynamically.

A finite state machine or transition system is usually required for many telecommunications switching systems. We have found that simply applying a state pattern achieves all the benefits of the home-grown complex solutions without most of the development costs. Basically, we are allowing virtual methods and the resulting jump tables produced by the compiler to provide what used to require detailed hand coding. Figure 2.10 illustrates an improved extensible structure.

The code now becomes something similar to the following:

```
LegoSystem::processColor
{
    color->process()
}
Red::process()
{
    redprocess();
}
Yellow::process()
{
    yellowprocess();
}
Green::process()
{
    greenprocess();
}
```

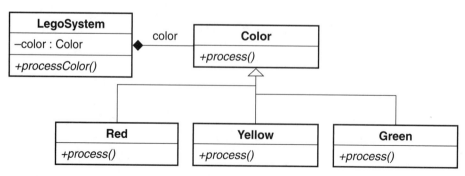

Figure 2.10 *An improved extensible structure*

Notice that we really haven't added any additional implementation code but rather have provided a support framework that allows us to graft on the additional colors easily. The real advantage increases when we combine multiple areas with case statements, allowing us to group the behavior into a common class; we can now easily add and modify state-specific behavior.

When we look at a large system, the key is to identify those points where future extension is likely to occur. For these, we can use patterns to act as "hinge points" in which new functionality can be added. Once we understand the variability we need, we find that we can utilize patterns to provide it.

Most important, by allowing us to provide this separation of the parts of the system, we can better handle multiple developers, testing, and distribution of systems. This book will address these issues throughout.

Training

As with most developers, I began my career working on existing systems, maintaining and extending them. The normal process I discovered when dealing with huge systems was to find a piece of code that sort of did what you wanted, copy it, and then tweak it to get the final product. I would like to pretend that with our understanding of reuse and framework development techniques today that this approach has been completely eliminated from any software shops. The problem was that developers understood *how* to do certain things but not really *why*. When the operating system evolved, obsolete code continued to be used and written, with no one really understanding why. Patterns solve this problem in part by providing a solution along with the context so that the "why" comes across along with the "how." The risk in applying a solution without understanding why it works is that it may be misapplied in inappropriate situations.

With the high amount of transition among IT professionals, the concern over knowledge transfer is paramount. Several efforts to capture the information assets are ongoing, including the creation of "Best Practices." For example, several telecommunications companies fear that new developers will not learn new lessons as the generation that built the original infrastructure begins to retire. The use of patterns is essential to capture this essential knowledge.

Silver Bullets

Let's get this out now and be done with it: Patterns are not the mystical silver bullet that will resolve all of our issues in software development. Instead, it is better to think of patterns as an essential tool to add to our arsenal. They can resolve many of our communication issues, provide a well-proven set of knowledge, and allow us to jump start many development activities.

Most important to consider is that patterns are relatively new. I include a brief time line of events and publications that illustrate this fact.

A Selected History of Patterns

1964   Christopher Alexander publishes *Notes on the Synthesis of Form* [Ale, 64], which attempts to look at the process of architecture in a different light.

1977   Christopher Alexander publishes *A Pattern Language* [Ale, 77].

1987   Ward Cunningham and Kent Beck begin applying some of the architectural concepts to software development in SmallTalk.

1992   Jim Coplien publishes *Advanced C++: Programming Style and Idioms* [Cop, 92].

1992   Peter Coad publishes his work on analysis patterns in *ACM* [Coa, 92].

1993   Erich Gamma's Ph.D. thesis with additional work from John Vlissides, Ralph Johnson, and Richard Helm is presented at ECOOP 93. This forms the basis of *Design Patterns*. [Gam, 93].

1993   Kent Beck, Grady Booch, Jim Coplien, and others formed the Hillside Group to provide a forum for discussion of patterns.

1994   First PLoP (Pattern Language of Programming) conference is held.

1994   *Design Patterns: Elements of Reusable Object-Oriented Software* is published. It is still considered by some to be the best OO book of all time.

1996   Frank Buschmann and others publish *Pattern-Oriented Software Architecture: A System of Patterns* [Bus, 96].

1997   Martin Fowler publishes *Analysis Patterns: Reusable Object Models*.

1999   Martin Fowler and others publish *Refactoring: Improving the Design of Existing Code* [Fow, 99].

2000   Linda Rising's *The Pattern Almanac* [Ris, 00], cataloging published patterns, is made available.

Summary

This chapter provides a quick overview of why patterns are an essential piece of any development effort providing the building blocks of system architecture. Not only do they provide canned knowledge to address recurring architectural problems, but they also provide a vocabulary in which to talk about design. We have shown how they allow us to provide for an extensible infrastructure and for the training of developers.

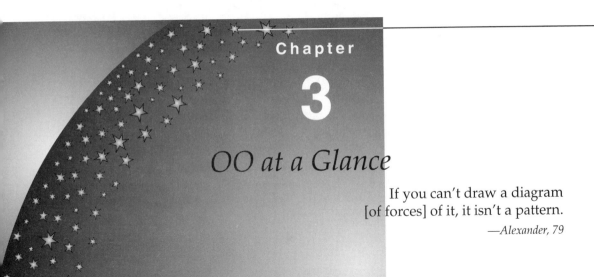

OO at a Glance

> If you can't draw a diagram
> [of forces] of it, it isn't a pattern.
>
> —*Alexander, 79*

Introduction

This chapter goes through some fundamental building blocks that we need in developing software systems. I will trace the evolution of the implementation modules that we use, utilizing the standardized Unified Modeling Language (UML) as a notation for documenting systems. More than a graphical notation, the UML defines the syntax and semantics to express concepts; thus it is actually a language. It is important that we lay the groundwork so that future chapters can ensure that we are all on the same footing and can use the same terminology to mean the same thing.

First let's look at the major program units as the software development practice has changed. Initially the major unit was simply the "program." See Figure 3.1. Harder problems resulted in larger programs.

As the size of the programs became harder to maintain, the idea of breaking them up into larger function units known as "modules" came into play. This resulted in structural and top-down design practices (Figure 3.2).

In the late 1960s, David Parnas made some observations about decomposing systems into modules. The key to creating less complex software, he observed, was to package functions and their data together. This was the basis of Encapsulation, an essential element to the development of OOD techniques. This resulted in the modeling of Abstract Data Types (ADT) (Figure 3.3),

---

SOAPBOX

It's hard for me to believe that it has been close to 15 years since I was involved in my first object-oriented proof of concepts (I tend to deal with getting older through denial). This was when many organizations were evaluating the use of objects through small projects to "prove" the technology. This approach (which in the last few years I've also seen applied to patterns) works fairly well, if the team doing the prototype project is knowledgeable in the correct application of the technology. Several organizations I worked with initially staffed these projects with people who had no real understanding of object technology; thus the evaluation showed that objects would not work in environment X.

I have seen similar things happen in recent years with patterns. One group I was involved with banned the use of patterns after one of the developers became so enamored with patterns that he attempted to use all 23 in a single program. Obviously this ignores the whole purpose of applying patterns based on context and really demonstrated the group's lack of knowledge. However, this resulted in management being very suspicious of patterns. It took quite a bit of effort on my part to undo this damage. I still recommend the proof of concept starter projects as a training experience, and I always recommend having an external expert involved in helping to jump start the efforts.

---

which formed the basis of Object-Based Design. This approach allowed the internal state or data to be hidden, limiting the access to operations that set or get the value of the state. This allows the representation of the data to vary without affecting any of the clients (or users) of the ADT. Operations are performed when a message is received from a client.

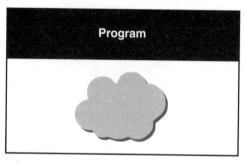

Figure 3.1   *A simple program*

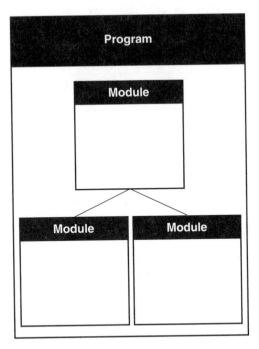

Figure 3.2   *Structured design*

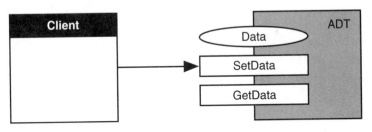

Figure 3.3   *Abstract Data Type*

We can then extend this concept by grouping a collection of related operations and by having this define the signature or "type," more commonly referred to as an "interface." This can be expressed in UML as a three-part rectangle showing the name (required), attributes (not normally in an interface), and operations (optional); as shown in Figure 3.4.

The interface defines only the signature. We then have to describe the implementation of this signature, which we can refer to as a "class." There may be

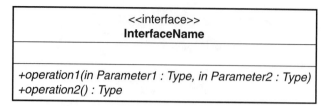

Figure 3.4 *Interface notation*

multiple classes that implement one or more interfaces; these can be expressed in UML in a way similar to an interface, as a three-part rectangle showing the name (required), attributes (optional), and operations (optional); as shown in Figure 3.5.

We can show that a class implements an interface in two ways. The first way uses a directed line from the class to the interface (Figure 3.6). This line is broken to show that it implements an interface (a solid line is used for class inheritance).

The second way to show a class implementing an interface is the canonical way in which interfaces implemented by the class or an other entity are shown using a lollipop-like extension (Figure 3.7).

Inheritance

Inheritance is a method to express generalization or "kind of" relationships. So if we say that Rectangle inherits from Shape, we are making a claim that a rectangle is a kind of shape.[1]

ClassName
−attribute1 : Type −attribute2 : Type
+operation1() : Type +operation2(in Parameter1 : Type)

Figure 3.5 *Class notation*

---

1. It is important in this discussion to recognize the difference between a mathematical definition and a programmatic one. Mathematically, a square is a rectangle. However, as we shall see shortly, programmatically it may not be as clear.

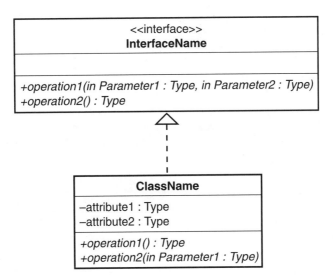

Figure 3.6 *A class implementing an interface*

I like to think about inheritance as fonts on a word processor. Most people recall the first document they created after discovering the ability to change fonts. It pretty much violated the first law of desktop publishing: Never make your document look like a ransom note. The nice thing about this phenomenon is that usually the first reader would mark it up and indicate that we were misusing this tool. Well, a similar thing happens with the use of inheritance. The code review process, much like the document review process, should have indicated that this is an incorrect use of the tool. Unfortunately, more often than not, the reviewer has no better idea of the proper use of the tool than the original coder does. The effect is serious misuses of inheritance that unfortunately cause much of the modeling and overall power of the tool to be lost.

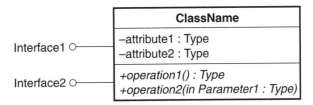

Figure 3.7 *Canonical form of implementing an interface*

Programming Languages

Recently I was surprised in a job interview I was conducting for a midlevel software engineer. The question I asked was, "How do you implement an interface in C++?" The answer that shocked me was, "C++ doesn't support interfaces; only Java does." It became very clear to me (as I continue to harp) that for many the conceptual understanding of the difference between design and direct language support is lacking. COBOL in its earliest version did not directly support structural programming, but techniques to use the language to support the model did emerge. In the case of C++ and Java, the language differences are not as great as people might think (although the OS/VM/Pcode differences that many don't quite get are!) Following is a simple set of concepts and how they are done in C++, or Java. It should also be clear that Java, which was developed after C++, is more semantically rich to express the common concepts used in C++. This semantic richness does make it easier for developers. For this reason, I think Java is a far superior teaching language, even if the end product is in C++.

	C++	**Java***
Interface	Use abstract classes	Use keyword interface
Class (Abstract)	Use some pure virtual function	Use keyword abstract with class (or any function)
Class (Concrete)	Use keyword class (no pure virtual functions)	Use keyword class (no abstract functions)
Parameterization	Use keyword template (or macros)	No language support (use common base object for many cases)

*We are concerning ourselves here only with the elements of addressing these key concepts. The far more profound differences between the languages come from things such as the Virtual Machine, Garbage Collection, and Libraries.

People generally miss the "proper" use of inheritance. Inheritance should be used only when it truly supports a "kind of" relationship. A good test for this correct usage is Liskov's substitution principle [Lis, 88]. Basically the concept is that inheritance is appropriate when a subclass (or subtype) or implementation class is interchangeable for a base class in each and every situation. In order to do this, the subclass cannot add any additional constraints that the parent does not have. Figure 3.8 illustrates a "bad" use of inheritance.

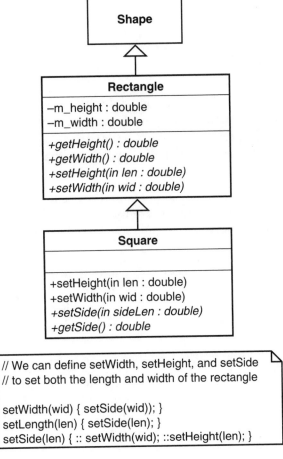

Figure 3.8   *A "bad" use of inheritance*

For example, a classic example is a square and a rectangle. We could define an operation on a square that implements length and width in terms of the side of the square.

All well and good, but now consider the following piece of pseudocode to increase the width of a rectangle until it is greater than its height:

```
void resize(Rectangle r)
{
while (r.getHeight() <= r.getWidth())
{
    r.setwidth(r.getWidth() + 1)
}
}
```

When we call this code for a rectangle, it works great, but when we pass it a square, it will not work the way we anticipate. The width will continue to increase until it overflows because the increase in the height is a side effect of our implementation. The problem is that a square is more constrained than a rectangle, which requires the sides to be of a different height; therefore we are faced with a dilemma. Either allow the square to set the height and width independently (which violates our definition of square), or document limitations on the use of the square. Unfortunately, either approach requires the caller of any function expecting a rectangle to understand all the details of what the operation will do. In effect, you have to violate the encapsulation we attempted to start with.

In addition, there are data elements present in the rectangle that are not part of the square. We are storing twice the required data (height + width vs. just side). This results in a general guideline when we work with inheritance hierarchies.

An important guideline when using inheritance is to put common code as high in the hierarchy as possible so it can be reused (unlike data elements, there is no additional cost per instance for code you are not using in the hierarchy), but keep data elements as low in the hierarchy as possible (see Figure 3.9). This will ensure you don't pay for data elements you don't use, but you get to maximize the use of common code.

A better solution would have been to create a common Polygon Class to provide the definition of abstract getHeight and getWidth methods that are common to all polygons (see Figure 3.10). Be sure (as noted earlier) to store the data elements in the lowest common denominator, in this case in the square and rectangle themselves.

Two other essential concepts are Abstract Classes and Concrete Classes. An Abstract Class defines a common base class that cannot be instantiated. This means that object instances that are the abstract class can be created. The abstract class can define only a base from which to derive other classes. A *concrete class* is any class that is not an abstract class so it may be used to create an instance. Abstract classes usually represent concepts or generalizations such as a shape or vehicle. Concrete classes usually represent more specific entities such as a square or a Toyota Celica.

While concrete classes can be inherited from, it should be done with care. Scott Meyers [Mey, 96] takes this concept so far as to say that concrete classes should never be inherited from. This matches the style that I prefer in implementing a framework because it provides the cleanest framework to allow later extension.

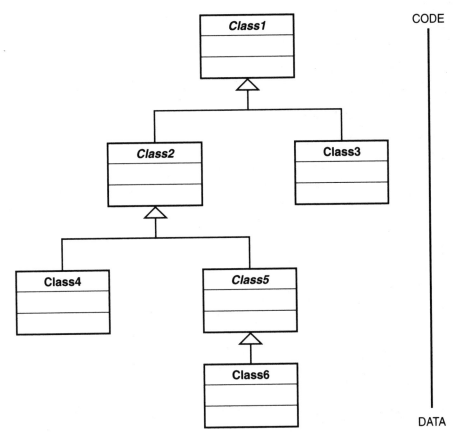

Figure 3.9 *Code should always be as high as possible in a hierarchy with the data at the bottom*

One other problem that inheritance imposes is that much of the encapsulation power of objects is lost, causing the implementer to be forced to understand the entire hierarchy. For example, in Figure 3.10, the implementer of Rectangle must understand the *implementation* of Shape and Quadralateral because they pay the related costs. In addition, this must be defined at compile time rather than at run time so if the implementer of a rectangle decides it wants to reuse portions of a different class instead, it is out of luck.

If inheritance is not always appropriate, then what is an alternative? Figure 3.11 illustrates a guideline for inheritance.

Using Composition (i.e., delegating the function calls) lends itself to a much better general structure, as shown in Figure 3.12.

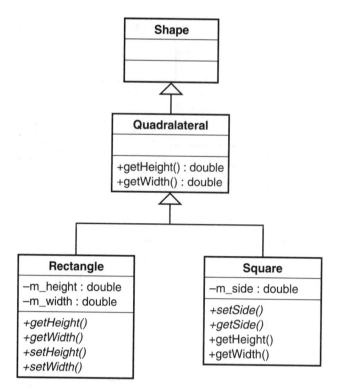

Figure 3.10   *A "better" use of inheritance*

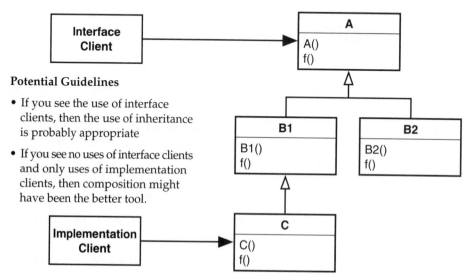

Potential Guidelines

- If you see the use of interface clients, then the use of inheritance is probably appropriate

- If you see no uses of interface clients and only uses of implementation clients, then composition might have been the better tool.

Figure 3.11   *A guideline for inheritance*

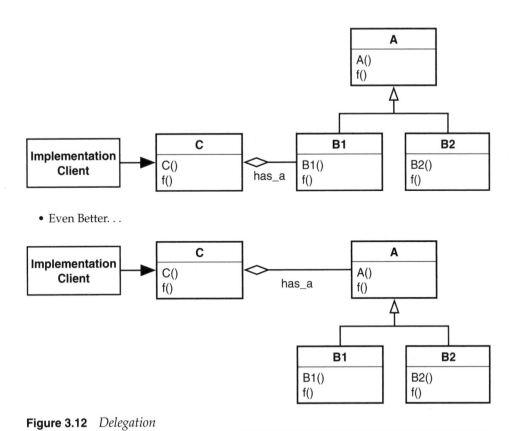

• Even Better. . .

Figure 3.12   *Delegation*

Components

As classes evolved, the idea of code reuse continued to become more challenging. It was recognized that a better unit of distribution was necessary, causing component distribution models to become more prevalent. In this approach an interface or a set of interfaces is exposed by a unit, which we will call a component. This approach can be implemented in a number of ways by bundling these components into shared libraries or executable units. This approach is supported by Microsoft's COM (which is evolving into the .NET framework) and OMG's CORBA middleware by coordinating communication and marshalling (converting data types and distribution). It is also supported by language-specific assemblies such as Enterprise Java Beans (EJB).

The current evolution is the addition of transactional support to allow components to participate in events that involve multiple components. Transaction Monitors are evolving both in Microsoft COM through MTS, as well as in vendor-specific solutions, including hybrid solutions taking traditional transac-

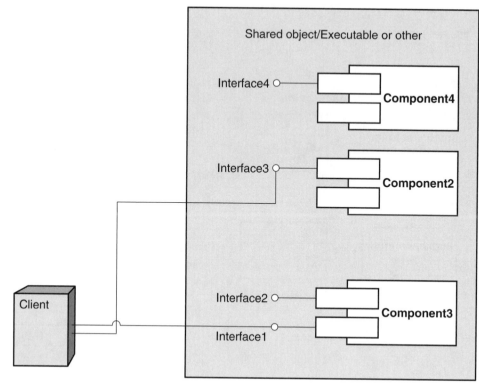

Figure 3.13   *Components*

tion monitors and proving a CORBA or Java layer (such as the BEA systems Jolt product). In addition, language-specific Java Application Servers are becoming more stable and are able to be used for high-end enterprise frameworks. Figure 3.13 illustrates some of these components.

Summary

In this chapter we discussed the evolution of the unit of composition of software systems—from the program as a whole to self-contained components that form a complex framework. In addition, we covered the basics of objects, inheritance, and composition. This basic vocabulary will allow us to take the next step in developing systems.

UML provides a semantically rich notation set that includes class diagrams, object diagrams, use case diagrams, sequence diagrams, collaboration diagrams, statechart diagrams, activity diagrams, component diagrams, and deployment diagrams. The proper diagram or set of diagrams to use at any given point depends on what you are hoping to express. In an overview chapter such as this, I can scarcely begin to do the UML justice. I recommend that developers start with *UML Distilled* by Martin Fowler [Fow, 97b] and then move on to the *UML Users Guide* by Grady Booch, et al [Boo, 99].

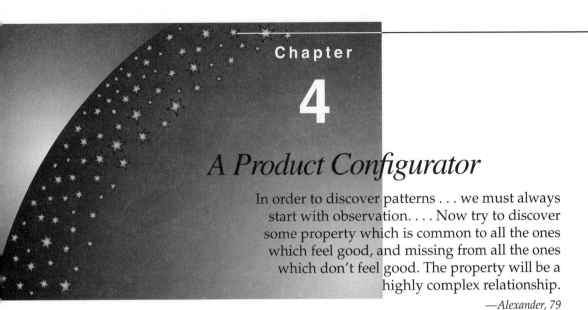

A Product Configurator

In order to discover patterns . . . we must always
start with observation. . . . Now try to discover
some property which is common to all the ones
which feel good, and missing from all the ones
which don't feel good. The property will be a
highly complex relationship.

—*Alexander, 79*

Introduction

Now we are ready to move on to a simple example. In this chapter we
develop a simple product configuration system. Our goal in building this system is to provide a framework that will allow us to develop and test a system
quickly. In addition, we will attempt to ensure that the design is readily able
to expand and extend the system.

Problem Definition

Consider a sales system that supports a sales representative selling a certain
kind of computer to end users.

Let's assume the base pieces are defined as in Table 4.1.

The sales person will sell a configuration for a computer such as that in
Table 4.2.

Table 4.1   *Computer Components*

Part	Choices
Motherboard + Processor	486, Pentium, PentiumII, Xeon, Pentium III
Case	Desktop, Minitower, Fulltower
Drives	4,6,10,13G
Memory	32M, 64M, 128M, 256M, 512M
Monitor	15", 17", 19", 21"
Soundcard	Regular, 3D
Video Card	Standard, Pro, 3D
Modem	None, 28K, 56K, ISDN

Table 4.2   *A Basic Computer System*

Galaxy Pro Computer System	
Motherboard + Processor	PentiumII
Case	Minitower
Drives	10G
Memory	64M
Monitor	17"
Soundcard	Regular
Video Card	Pro
Modem	28K
Price	**$1800**

One approach might be to model this computer system as a simple representation of an object that we can sell that contains parts that can be selected (see Figure 4.1). As I show later, this approach is extremely rigid and hampers the ability to extend the system in the future.

We want a way for the sales department to come up with a configuration from these items and to be able to select them from a list of products. In addition, as new parts are added, we want to be able to add them rapidly to our deployments.

Now let's change the implementation of the Soundboard Class to support a new type of soundcard. This requires first changing the Soundboard Class and potentially breaking any existing code (violating the Open-Closed Principle

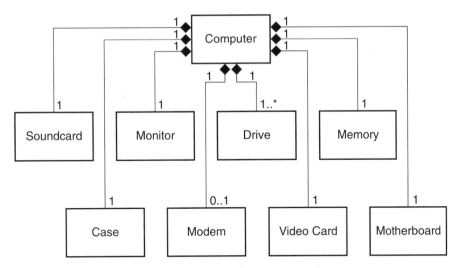

Figure 4.1 *A representative model of the product configuration*

discussed earlier, or more simply, if it ain't broke, don't touch it) or creating a new class. If the change results in even a minor change to the interface (for example, adding a single new data member), this will cause a ripple effect since the Computer Class must also change. In effect, any change (no matter how small) will force a rebuild and will potentially ripple throughout the entire code base. Basically, we are generating too many classes that are far too rigid. What we need is a better way.

Solution

Let's consider a simple framework to allow additional prices for a setup and reconfiguration by parts. We would also like to be able to display a description/invoice of parts. This framework will be more than a simple select from a product list; it should allow us to ensure that a valid configuration is built. Let's start by considering the major entities:

Parts: A part is an entity that may be sold.

1. All parts consume and provide resources.
2. All parts have a name.
3. All parts have a description.
4. All parts have a price (either fixed or set by an algorithm).
5. Complex parts may be composed of other parts.

Resources: A resource is any entity that is provided or consumed by a part.

1. A resource has a name.

2. A resource has a quantity.

Configuration: A configuration is a valid set of parts that can be sold.

1. Configurations consume and provide resources.

2. Configurations have a name.

3. Configurations have a description.

4. Configurations have a price.

Observations

Let's start by looking at the part concept (although we will be observing the same concepts for resources and configurations). After the base attributes, the first thing we might see is that parts can be treated as an individual part or as a group of parts.

For example, I might sell a configured motherboard with a processor installed, or I might sell the processor and the motherboard separately.

The naive way would be to require clients to test each part to determine whether it is a group or an individual part. For example, a routine to calculate the part price might have to do something like the following:

```
Amount GetPartPrice(part)
{
    If (part.style = GROUP) then
        // loop through each child and check if
        // it is a group, if so recursively apply
        // to each child
    else
        // get price

    return price;
}
```

This is not ideal because we now require the clients to ask information about the implementation or structure of the object. We would like to be able to avoid having the clients use them uniformly without worrying about the exact implementation we are using. This is where a Composite Pattern [Gam, 95] comes to our aid.

Composite

Intent

The intent is to compose objects into tree structures to represent part/whole hierarchies. Composite lets clients treat individual objects and compositions of objects uniformly.

Varies

Varies includes the structure and composition of an object.

Structure

The composite structure is shown in Figure 4.2.

Comments

Composite is probably one of the most highly used patterns. The key to this pattern is the uniform treatment of part/whole hierarchies; simply supporting a tree structure doesn't cut it unless clients are completely free from the knowledge of whether they are dealing with a leaf or a composite node.

The Composite pattern allows us to model a hierarchy without requiring the users of the components to have any special case logic to determine if they are dealing with a simple item or a group of items.

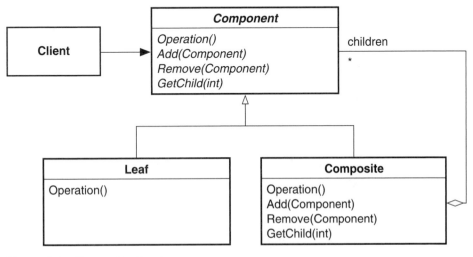

Figure 4.2 *Composite structure*

Let's take a quick look at how we would apply a Composite pattern here. First note a few things about this class diagram. We have created a simple base class (part) to provide a common interface for clients. As we mentioned earlier, we would use a composite pattern to create two concrete classes (recall that concrete classes are those classes that we allow to be created), called SimplePart and CompositePart. The only difficult decision that results is what to do with the AddPart and RemovePart members. When using the composite, we are faced with either leaving it in the base class and deciding some valid meaning for the SimplePart or requiring clients to know they are dealing with the CompositePart when they call these operations. I chose to place it in the base and have the SimplePart throw an exception, indicating an error if it is invoked.

The composite part turned out to be interesting since the pricing model might be a special price (package deal) or a summation of its parts. My initial thoughts were to implement the pricing model using a State Pattern to vary the pricing based on the mode of the composite (see the section State Pattern in Chapter 2, "An Introduction to Patterns"). That would allow the pricing model to be externalized and be even more flexible. However, I have only two models and can't think of a third necessary item for this model. I decide to keep it simple and use a raw implementation. There are only two pricing options now, but when or if a third pricing option creates itself, I will employ the State Pattern.

One other question the careful observer might ask is: Why use BasicPart? Simple; I believe that data members should never be present in a base class. Introducing a middle class provides the data members to the simple and composite parts. If all classes have the data members, why not introduce them in the parent class?

To use one example, suppose I want to introduce a trace logging capability to my system. This could be done by using a Decorator Pattern (for an example of decorator see page 66) that would simply echo messages to an output device and then call the wrapped parent part. By introducing a simple class, I could add tracing to the entire hierarchy, but this wrapper does not need a separate name, description, or so on. If I had placed the data members in Part, it would have to pay for it anyway. Again, always place data members as low in the hierarchy as possible; place functional members high in the hierarchy (functional members don't incur costs on children). See Figure 4.3 for an illustration of Part hierarchy.

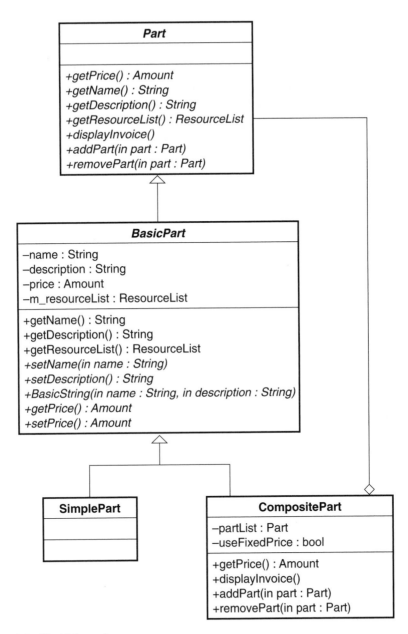

Figure 4.3 *Part hierarchy*

Now let's consider the resources (see Figure 4.4). I started approaching this the same way as I did with parts, Resources should uniformly be able to deal with simple and complex objects, so we could again introduce a Composite

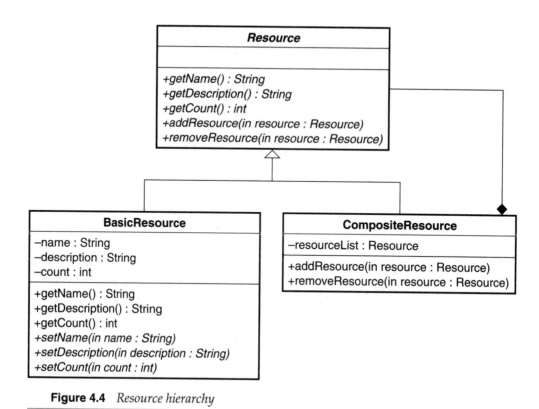

Figure 4.4 *Resource hierarchy*

Pattern. We could allow resources to be combined and subtracted from each other simply by adjusting the count on named objects appropriately. These are all things we *could* do, but when I began implementation, I realized that this was overkill, and a simple class ResourceList (Figure 4.5) met our requirements. Remember that usually the simple solutions are best so don't be afraid to throw your work out if it makes things better.

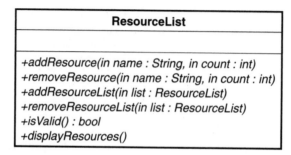

Figure 4.5 *ResourceList*

The configuration object (when we look at the requirements) can now be viewed as a Composite Part that has a valid configuration (i.e., no resources with a negative count). This is my favorite type of coding—the kind we don't have to do at all.

To make things a little easier to manage, I created a simple PartList object whose purpose was to store a list of parts by name for easy lookup. Putting this all together results in the following illustration (Figure 4.6):

The code for this is fairly straightforward. The main subroutine follows (see Appendix A: Product Code for the complete code):

```
/**
 * Test Driver Main - Creates a simple configuration and outputs it.
 *
 */
public static void main (String[] args)
{
    PartList list = new PartList();
    fillPartList(list);
    Part base = new CompositePart("Galaxy Pro
200","Basic setup system");
    base.addPart(list.getPart("BBC1"));
    base.addPart(list.getPart("D256"));
    base.displayInvoice(System.out, 0);
    System.out.println("Resource are: " +
(base.getResourceList().isValid() ? "Valid" : "Invalid"));
    base.getResourceList().displayResources(System.out);
}
```

The program results in the following output:

```
Galaxy Pro 200:Basic setup system:570.0
    BBC1:BareBones Config 1:300.0
        Sota24:Sota 24:115.0
        I550:550Mhz Slot 1 Processor:300.0
        MX24:Std Mid-sized Tower Case:59.0
    D256:256MB Dimm Memory - 1 slot:270.0
Resource are: Valid
Motherboard: 0
DIMM: 2
Slot 1: 0
PCI Slots: 5
```

The core framework seems pretty straightforward. Looking at the test driver program (Driver.java), we can easily see that adding parts to the list is a bit more of a pain for the end user than we would like. What would be great is a better way in which to create the configuration objects, specifically to avoid

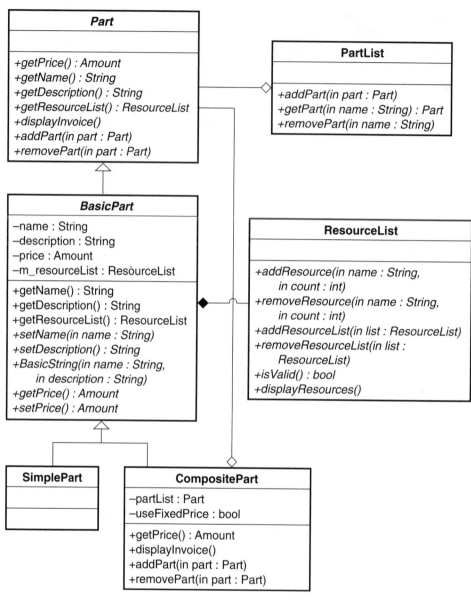

Figure 4.6 *Updated part structure*

direct coupling with the implementation classes and to hide end-user knowledge of simple vs. composite objects. For this, a creational pattern should be added. Because building a part can be a complex series of steps, I will use a Builder Pattern [Gam, 95], as in Figure 4.7.

▓ ▓ ▓ ▓

Builder Pattern

Intent

Separate the construction of a complex object from its representation so that the same construction process can create different representations.

Varies

This step includes how a composite object is created.

Structure

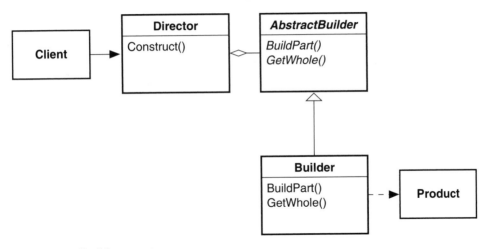

Figure 4.7 *Builder structure*

Comments

By separating the construction and assembly process, complex rules to ensure that the client can easily assemble composite objects can be added.

Normally whenever a composite, decorator, or chain of responsibility is in place, consider whether a builder is called for.

▓ ▓ ▓ ▓

In the example shown in Figure 4.8, this is done as follows:

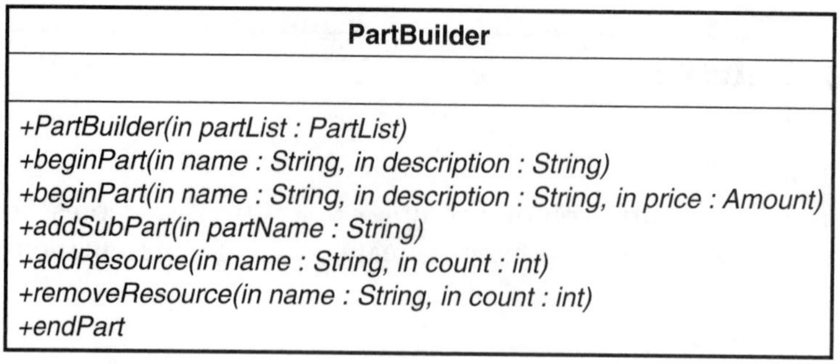

PartBuilder
+PartBuilder(in partList : PartList)
+beginPart(in name : String, in description : String)
+beginPart(in name : String, in description : String, in price : Amount)
+addSubPart(in partName : String)
+addResource(in name : String, in count : int)
+removeResource(in name : String, in count : int)
+endPart

Figure 4.8   *Part builder*

Coding this new routine is relatively straightforward (see Appendix B: Product Code) and simplifies the main driver as follows:

driver.java

```
package ProductConfig;
public class Driver
{

public static void fillPartList(PartBuilder builder)
{
    builder.beginPart("Aplo2", "Apollo 2 Motherboard",109);
        builder.addResource("PCI Slots",5);
        builder.addResource("DIMM",3);
        builder.addResource("AGP Port",1);
        builder.addResource("Slot 1",1);
        builder.removeResource("Motherboard",1);
    builder.endPart();

    builder.beginPart("Sota24", "Sota 24",115);
        builder.addResource("PCI Slots",5);
        builder.addResource("DIMM",3);
        builder.addResource("Slot 1",1);
        builder.removeResource("Motherboard",1);
    builder.endPart();

    builder.beginPart("MX24","Std Mid-sized Tower Case",59);
        builder.addResource("Motherboard",1);
    builder.endPart();

    builder.beginPart("FX24","Std Full-sized Tower Case",79);
        builder.addResource("Motherboard",1);
    builder.endPart();
```

```
        builder.beginPart("I550","550Mhz Slot 1 Processor",300);
            builder.removeResource("Slot 1",1);
        builder.endPart();

        builder.beginPart("I600","600Mhz Slot 1 Processor",350);
            builder.removeResource("Slot 1",1);
        builder.endPart();

        builder.beginPart("D128","128MB Dimm Memory",120);
            builder.removeResource("DIMM",1);
        builder.endPart();

        builder.beginPart("D256","256MB Dimm Memory - 1 slot",270);
            builder.removeResource("DIMM",1);
        builder.endPart();

        builder.beginPart("D256-2","256MB Dimm Memory - 2 slots",230);
            builder.removeResource("DIMM",2);
        builder.endPart();

        builder.beginPart("BBC1","BareBones Config 1",300);
            builder.addSubPart("Sota24");
            builder.addSubPart("I550");
            builder.addSubPart("MX24");
        builder.endPart();

    }

    public static void main (String[] args)
    {
        PartList list = new PartList();
        PartBuilder builder = new PartBuilder(list);

        fillPartList(builder);
        builder.beginPart("Galaxy Pro 200","Basic setup system");
            builder.addSubPart("BBC1");
            builder.addSubPart("D256");
        builder.endPart();
        Part base = list.getPart("Galaxy Pro 200");
        base.displayInvoice(System.out, 0);
        System.out.println("Resource are: " +
            (base.getResourceList().isValid() ?
                "Valid" : "Invalid"));
        base.getResourceList().displayResources(System.out);
    }

}
```

The final structure now looks like the product Configuration System in Figure 4.9.

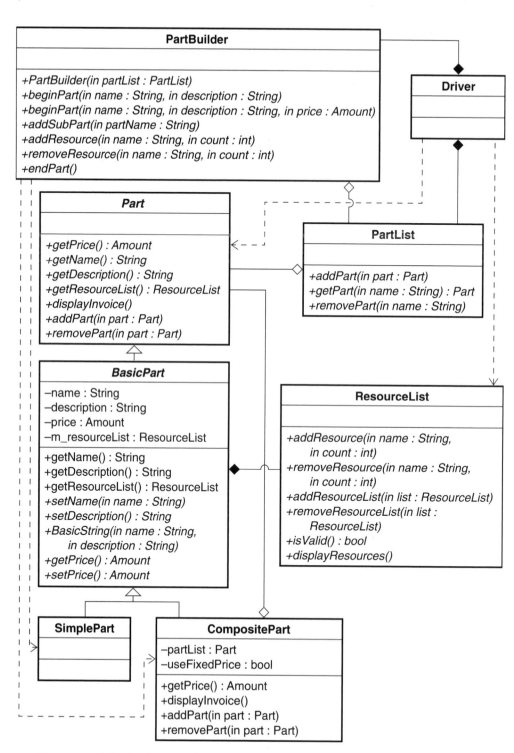

Figure 4.9 *The Product Configuration System*

Note that the only dependent on SimplePart or CompositePart is the builder. This means that clients can begin utilizing the Part interface while the hierarchy of Part and Builder are being developed. This type of structure lends itself nicely to parallel development. It also makes testing and modifying existing code easier.

Sample

In the example in this chapter we took a pretty straightforward approach to providing a Product Configuration System by applying abstraction and then utilizing a few simple patterns. Note that we also took advantage of several patterns provided within the Java language itself. The Enumerator used throughout this example is a language-provided Iterator (which provides a way to access all the elements of a composite structure). The final solution, though, is far from perfect, but it provides a good first pass in which to begin the system.

BurgerShop 101

No matter what method is used, the pattern is an
attempt to discover some invariant feature,
which distinguishes good places from bad places
with respect to some particular system of forces.

—Alexander, 79

Overview

In this chapter I will walk through a small example from beginning to end to show how a pattern can be used to solve a common problem, namely class explosion, in object-oriented design.

Sue's Burger Shop

Consider a fictional restaurant called Sue's Burger Shop. Let's assume for purposes of simplicity that the shop sells only burgers. Let's model this simply as a burger and start from there. Furthermore, I'm going to assume that you've been awake until this point and you understand that an interface for a base class is a great idea here. So let's model the basic burger in terms of a sandwich (operations such as purchase, eat, and so on are suppressed). See Figure 5.1.

Now we decide that we want to sell Cheeseburgers as well (see Figure 5.2). Hmm, inheritance to the rescue. . .

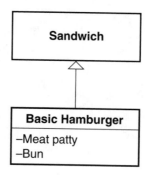

Figure 5.1 *The hamburger hierarchy*

Wow! That was pretty easy; that is, until we have to support onions on the burger *and* on the cheeseburger. Let's use our trusty inheritance tool (see Figure 5.3) for that as well.

Okay, having to add two classes is a little annoying, but fine, we can cope. The astute reader can guess what's coming next—tomatoes! So, using our tool du jour, inheritance, we now also support hamburger with tomato, hamburger

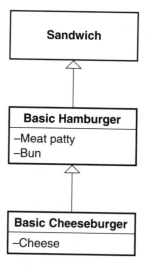

Figure 5.2 *Extending to include cheeseburgers*

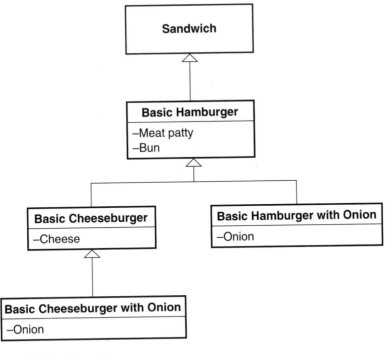

Figure 5.3 *Adding the onions*

with tomato and onion, cheeseburger with tomato, and cheeseburger with tomato and onion. See Figure 5.4.

Four more classes is more than a little annoying! But now let's throw in lettuce. See Figure 5.5.

Wow, eight more classes! How many classes do you think it would be when we add the option for ketchup? If you guessed 16, you are there! How about mayonnaise? 32! Now bacon, 64! Salsa, 128! What we are seeing is an exponential number of classes. Yes, each one is trivial, but consider a single operation added to the mix: getPrice(). If we needed to add 5 cents to the price of any cheese order, there might be hundreds of places that would potentially be affected. This is clearly a violation of the single point of maintenance we were striving for earlier. You may think this example is a stretch, but most developers have seen this sort of problem evolve. It is usually handled simply by not supporting the entire set of options. For example, it would be like telling customers they can have onions only on cheeseburgers, not on hamburgers.

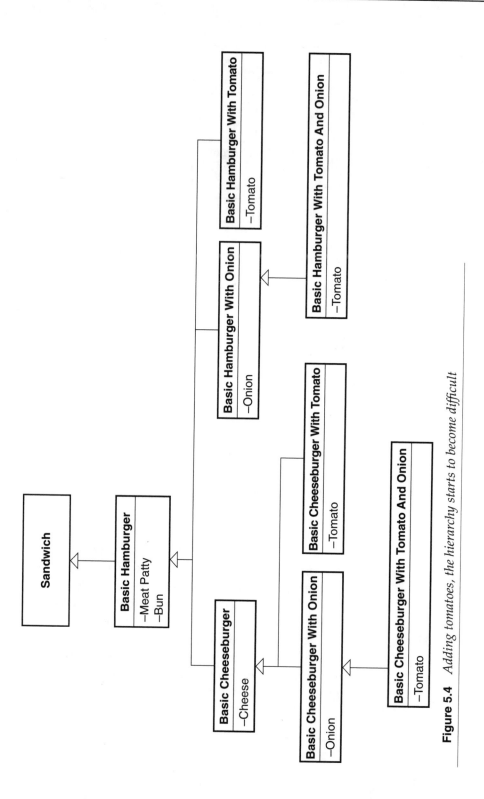

Figure 5.4 *Adding tomatoes, the hierarchy starts to become difficult*

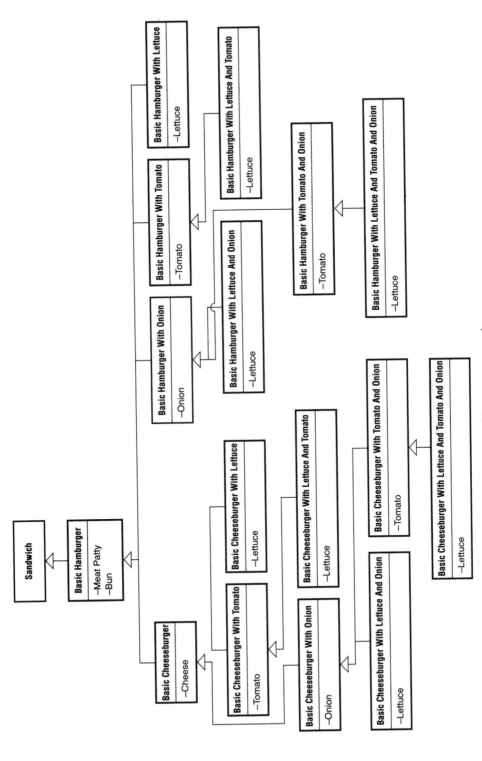

Figure 5.5 *Throwing in the lettuce, we now make things more complex*

Does it work like this in the real world? Usually not (although as we mentioned earlier, this happens more often than not in the coding world). Let's think about the problem a little differently; let's try to treat each of these toppings as just that, an add-on or decoration to the basic hamburger or, for that matter, to sandwiches in general.

Let's start again with our basic structure, but now let's allow a subclass of the sandwich that we will call a SandwichDecorator (see Figure 5.6). The decorator can simply decorate or wrap or top a sandwich so it will reference a sandwich. All the decorator will do is forward or delegate all operations to the sandwich that it wraps. In this case, getPrice() will simply call getPrice() of the wrapped sandwich.

This is pretty straighforward—this is also pretty useless. However, with this model let's consider the first topping: cheese. We use inheritance to indicate that it is a kind of decorator, as shown in Figure 5.7.

Notice that the getPrice operation calls the SandwichDecorator, which simply calls getPrice on the sandwich it decorates (see Figure 5.8). So to create a cheeseburger, we would perform the following steps:

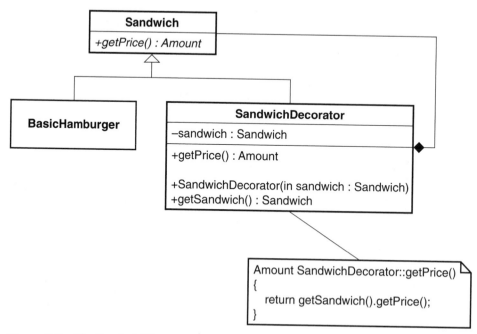

Figure 5.6   *The SandwichDecorator*

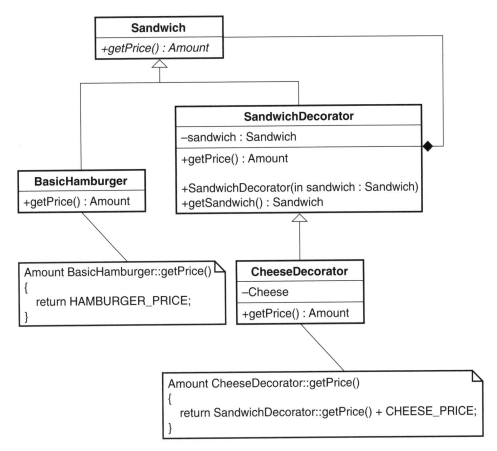

Figure 5.7 *Adding the CheeseDecorator*

```
Create a hamburger
BasicHamburger h;
Create a CheeseDecorator that decorates a hamburger
Sandwich s = new CheeseDecorator(h)

Calling getPrice on the sandwich would first call
CheeseDecorator::getPrice(),
   which would then call its base operation
SandwichDecorator::getPrice,
       which would then call BasicHamburger getPrice() returning
HAMBURGER_PRICE
          which would be added to CHEESE_PRICE,
   returning HAMBURGER_PRICE + CHEESE_PRICE.
```

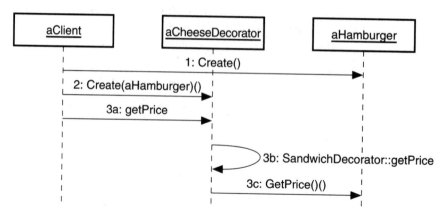

Figure 5.8 *Interaction diagram for calling getPrice*

Now let's extend this model to include onions, as shown in Figure 5.9.

At first it would seem that we would have to create an OnionDecorator as well as a CheeseAndOnionDecorator, but a CheeseDecorator inherits from Sandwich, so an OnionDecorator could, in fact, decorate a CheeseDecorator.

So, to support a burger with cheese and onions, we would create it as follows (using a compressed syntax):

```
Sandwich s = new OnionDecorator(new CheeseDecorator(new
BasicHamburger).

Invoking s->getPrice() would first call the oniondecorators
getPrice()
which would call its base getPrice() which would call its wrapped
getPrice()
which would call the CheeseDecorator getPrice
which would call its base getPrice() which would call its wrapped
getPrice()
which would call the BasicHamburger getPrice()
which would return HAMBURGER_PRICE
which would return HAMBURGER_PRICE + CHEESEBURGER_PRICE
which would return HAMBURGER_PRICE + CHEESEBURGER_PRICE +
        ONION_PRICE!
```

Trust me![1]

---

1. Believe it or not, the topic of using onions in this example was actually a point of contention because many places charge nothing for them (that is, *getPrice* returns 0). However, at my local establishment, onions (caramelized, fried, or otherwise) have an additional charge, which irks me a bit, so it provided a reasonable choice.

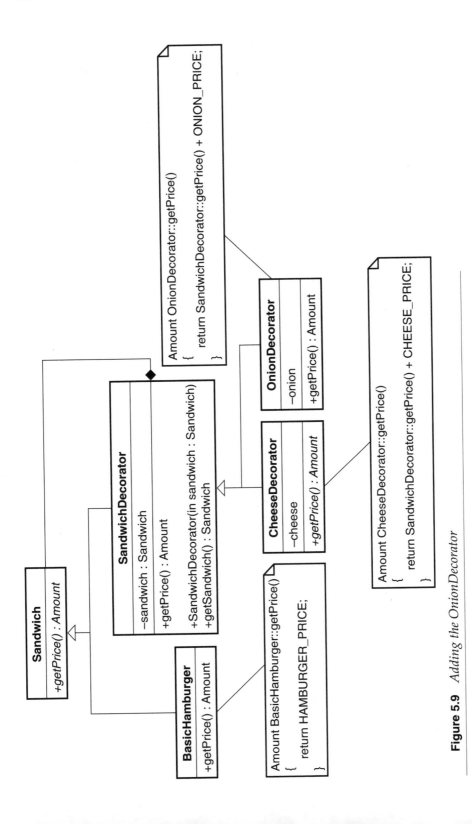

Figure 5.9 *Adding the OnionDecorator*

Now, how many additional classes are needed to support all these toppings? The basic hamburger and decorator bring it to 10 classes (see Figure 5.10)! A far cry from the (4+8+16+32+64+128) 252 classes discussed earlier.

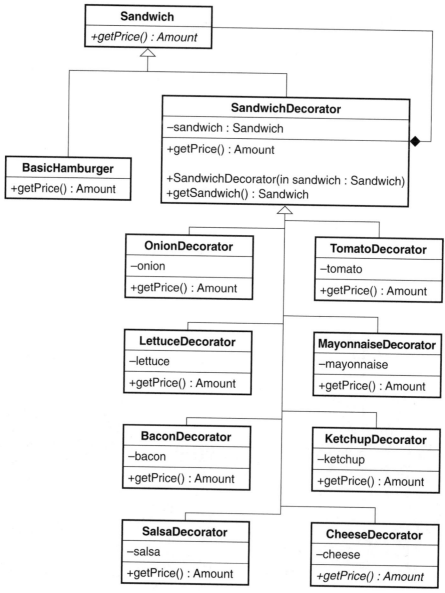

Figure 5.10   *Adding the toppings without class explosion*

For the complete sample code for this example in C++, see Appendix B: BurgerShop Code.

The main routine follows. Figure 5.11 illustrates the sample Burgerland program execution.

```
Main
// BurgerLand.cpp : Defines the entry point for the console
      application.
//
#include <iostream>
#include <memory>

#include "Sandwich.h"
#include "CheeseDecorator.h"
#include "BaconDecorator.h"
#include "TomatoDecorator.h"
#include "BasicHamburger.h"

int main(int argc, char* argv[])
{
    Sandwich* sand = new CheeseDecorator(new
        BaconDecorator(new TomatoDecorator(new BasicHamburger)));
std::cout << sand->getName() << " price = $" << sand->getPrice();
    delete sand;
return 0;
}
```

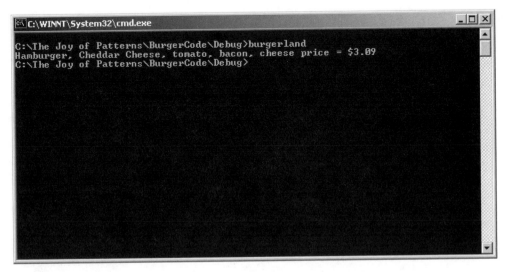

Figure 5.11 *Sample Burgerland program execution*

Reflections

We have accomplished turning an exponential problem into a linear problem; one more topping equals one more class. Furthermore, to change the implementation of the cheese topping (price, vendor, whatever) would simply involve a single point of maintenance.

Notice that we can support all the toppings architecturally without implementing all of them. In addition, we can place multiple developers on this framework without their stepping on each other's toes. One great benefit of this is that testing can also be done in isolation; changes to subclasses usually do not impact the testing already done to other subclasses.

Creating any variation of toppings (even adding double cheese) can be done simply by creating the decorators around the appropriate hamburger. This can get somewhat ugly for the client as the number of decorators increases. However, the bigger issue is that this assumes that there are no rules on the order in which these toppings are to be added. (I know I don't want the tomatoes placed between the meat patty and the cheese—yuck!) We often want to combine the Decorator Pattern with a Builder pattern. In this case we assign the rules assembly to a Builder class, which then attaches the toppings in the appropriate order (see Figure 5.12).

To build a bacon cheeseburger, a client would simply call something similar to the following code:

```
BurgerBuilder bb;
bb.startSandwich();
bb.addBacon();
bb.addCheese();
Sandwich s = bb.getSandwich();
```

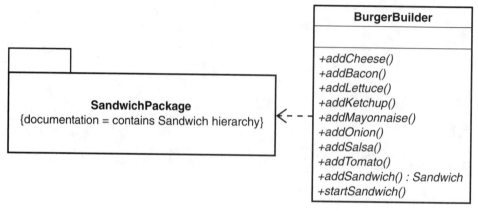

Figure 5.12   *Adding a Builder*

And the BurgerBuilder would ensure that the bacon is on top of the cheese.

Simplifications

Although this is an extreme example (and then some), it does illustrate the power of the decorator pattern. Obviously, the code of this application could be greatly reduced through parameterization of price and name—if that was the only variance. Suppose, however, that some of the decorators were not quite so simple. Perhaps some prices vary based on an inventory level or computed value. We would like to keep the core framework in place but avoid coding each of the decorator variations that differ only by name and price. This can be done simply by adding a template approach to handle the base case and yet still permit us to specialize other cases. In this way a reduction in code can result by unifying behavior where possible.

An example of a simple template definition to avoid coding the many classes is shown here:

```
/////////////////////////////////////////////////////////////
// TSandwichDecorator.h: interface for the Standard Template
        Decorator class.
/////////////////////////////////////////////////////////////
#if
        !defined(AFX_TSANDWICHDECORATOR_H__675D6594_481A_11D3_B
        A98_00500428B24D__INCLUDED_)
#define
        AFX_TSANDWICHDECORATOR_H__675D6594_481A_11D3_BA98_00500
        428B24D__INCLUDED_

#if _MSC_VER > 1000
#pragma once
#endif // _MSC_VER > 1000

#include "SandwichDecorator.h"

template <const Amount price>
class TSandwichDecorator : public SandwichDecorator
{
public:
inline TSandwichDecorator(const string& name, Sandwich* sandwich);
inline virtual ~TSandwichDecorator();
    inline virtual string getName();
    inline virtual Amount getPrice();
private:
    const string m_name;
};
```

```
template <const Amount price>
inline TSandwichDecorator<price>::TSandwichDecorator(const
      string& name, Sandwich* sandwich):
   SandwichDecorator(sandwich), m_name(name)
{

}

template <const Amount price>
inline TSandwichDecorator<price>::~TSandwichDecorator()
{

}

template <const Amount price>
inline string TSandwichDecorator<price>::getName()
{
    return getSandwich().getName() + ", " + m_name;
}

template <const Amount price>
inline Amount TSandwichDecorator<price>::getPrice()
{
    // current price - here for now - future calc
    return getSandwich().getPrice() + price;
}


#endif //
      !defined(AFX_TSANDWICHDECORATOR_H__675D6594_481A_11D3_B
      A98_00500428B24D__INCLUDED_)
```

This could then be used as follows:

```
// BurgerLandWithTemplate.cpp : Defines the entry point for
      the console application.
//
#include <iostream>
#include <memory>

#include "Sandwich.h"
#include "CheeseDecorator.h"
#include "BaconDecorator.h"
#include "TomatoDecorator.h"
#include "BasicHamburger.h"
#include "TSandwichDecorator.h"

static const string cheddarName = "Cheddar Cheese";
typedef TSandwichDecorator<.50> CheddarCheeseDecorator;
```

```
int main(int argc, char* argv[])
{
    Sandwich* sand = new CheeseDecorator(new
        BaconDecorator(new TomatoDecorator(new
        CheddarCheeseDecorator(cheddarName, new BasicHamburger)))));
std::cout << sand->getName() << " price = $" << sand->getPrice();
    delete sand;
return 0;
}
```

Summary

Whenever you use a decorator, be careful not to misuse; the number of function calls and complexity might be an issue in some domains. Be sure to determine if a strategy pattern (see GOF), often combined with a composite (also GOF), might be a better choice for altering sets of algorithms.

Here are some other things to think about:

- If we wished to add a new ChickenBurger type, how much of an impact to the existing system would result? How many toppings would it support? Compare this to the pure inheritance way to solve the problem.
- When I put together this problem, I considered making the meat patty itself a topping. What are the pros and cons to this approach?
- One problem with this solution is that the pricing factors are hardcoded into the classes, requiring a recompilation whenever prices change. Consider replacing this; read it from a database or from another configuration source (perhaps XML-based).

Programming Languages and Patterns

If we want a language which is deep and powerful, we can only have it under conditions where thousands of people are using the same language, exploring it, making it deeper all the time. And this can only happen when the languages are shared.

—Alexander, 79

Patterns are programming-language independent (as opposed to idioms that are programming-language specific). In a way, patterns form a language that are a step above the programming language in order to communicate other concepts such as design. This said, it is important to recognize that the specific programming language does play a significant part in the evolution of a software system. This is becoming true as programming languages today are more than simply language syntax and semantics. We must now consider the utilities, the libraries, and the general environment they provide—especially when we consider recent languages like Java or C#. These languages not only provide the traditional programming language syntax but are also built on a virtual machine and come complete with a rich set of libraries or packages to make development and reuse easier.

While any design pattern (by definition) can be implemented in any language, certain patterns are easier to implement in some languages than in others. For example, if the pattern builds on the use of multiple threads of control, it is a bit harder to convey this within the boundaries of C++ or Visual Basic than in Java. That said, by extending C++ with a thread library (such as Pthreads) or using low-level windows calls in Visual Basic, we can still accomplish these things—but not quite as easily.

In order to consider a design choice properly, we must include the programming language and development environments in the context we use to evaluate the design alternatives. Although it does not normally occur for a variety of organizational and training issues (as well as marketing issues), where possible the programming language selection should be done as part of design iterations. Understand, though, that it may enable certain design solutions to be implemented far more easily.

While systems developed using multiple languages should be considered, this may also create training and maintenance issues. For example, it is very common to see a system seamlessly using Visual Basic for the front-end presentation layer but utilizing C++ for the business layer and Transact-SQL (or PL-SQL) for the database layer. This important separation of tiers is actually enhanced by the separation of languages, but in these cases developers tend to focus on a single tier so that the training issues (and general confusion) are reduced. As virtual machines (such as Microsoft's .NET framework) evolve, this focus may be less of an issue in the future.

SOAPBOX

The original COBOL did not provide support for structured programming as a language construct, yet people managed to design and implement as structured programming became the rage. C does not provide language constructs to make object-oriented design easy, yet several object-oriented designs that were implemented in C that I have been fortunate enough to work with utilized the features it did provide to create an extremely efficient and elegant implementation. As design techniques evolve, language constructs and libraries to support different paradigms will also evolve. This does not imply that there will ever be a language rich enough to encompass all of the patterns or general approaches we require in design. Instead, it is my hope that as our vocabulary improves, the ease in which we can express complex designs will also improve.

Let's look at a specific example. Often in software we need to handle multiple objects that are dependent on the state of another object. For example, in an accounting system you may provide multiple views of the data, perhaps even multiple spreadsheet views as well as multiple graphical views. Whenever you change the data in one spreadsheet, the user would reasonably expect the other views to change (automatically, without selecting a refresh option). Patterns, though, transcend a specific domain. For example, in an embedded system you may have a similar problem of having multiple objects (such as monitors) watching a piece of hardware (through its software encapsulation/

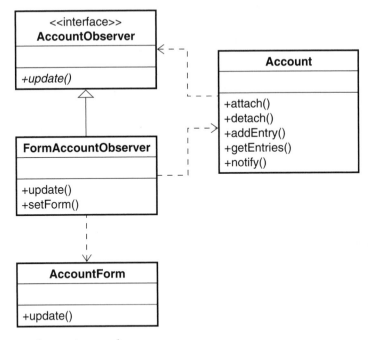

Figure 6.1 *Account example*

device driver) that have to react quickly when an interrupt, such as low power, occurs. A pattern can describe this situation and address how to proceed in a readily transferable manner. For example, this monitoring approach is described as the Observer Pattern [Gam, 95], discussed earlier in Chapter 2 ("Observer Pattern" on page 8).

Let's look at a simple model of this pattern. Consider an account (serving as a subject) that allows multiple observers. See Figure 6.1.

First let's look at implementing this solution in Visual Basic, a language not well known for its ability to handle object-oriented paradigms. As you can see, Visual Basic is more than capable of supporting the following pattern:

AccountForm

```
Option Explicit
Dim observer As FormAccountObserver

Public Sub update(modifiedAccount As Account)
    Dim currentEntry As accountEntry
    lstEntries.Clear
```

```
        For Each currentEntry In modifiedAccount.getEntries
            lstEntries.AddItem (currentEntry.entryDate & vbTab &
            currentEntry.amount)
        Next
    End Sub


    Private Sub cmdAdd_Click()
        Call testAccount.addEntry(txtDate, txtAmount)
        Call update(testAccount)
    End Sub



    Private Sub cmdSpawn_Click()
        Dim frm As New frmAccount
        frm.Show
    End Sub

    Private Sub cmdSync_Click()
        testAccount.notify
    End Sub

    Private Sub Form_Load()
        txtDate = Now()
        Set observer = New FormAccountObserver
        Call observer.setForm(Me)
        Call testAccount.attachObserver(observer, CStr(Me.hWnd))
        Call update(testAccount)
    End Sub


    Private Sub Form_Unload(Cancel As Integer)
        Call testAccount.detachObserver(observer, CStr(Me.hWnd))
    End Sub
```

Account

```
Option Explicit
Private mvarAccountEntryCollection As Collection
Private mvarObserverCollection As Collection
Private mvaraccountName As String

Public Property Let accountName(ByVal vData As String)
    mvaraccountName = vData
End Property

Public Property Get accountName() As String
    accountName = mvaraccountName
End Property

Public Function getEntries() As Collection
    Set getEntries = mvarAccountEntryCollection
End Function
```

```
Public Sub addEntry(entryDate As Date, amount As Currency)
    Dim entry As New accountEntry
    entry.amount = amount
    entry.entryDate = entryDate
    Call mvarAccountEntryCollection.Add(entry)
End Sub

Public Sub notify()
    Dim observer As AccountObserver
    For Each observer In mvarObserverCollection
        Call observer.update(Me)
    Next
End Sub

Public Sub detachObserver(observer As AccountObserver, key As
        String)
    Call mvarObserverCollection.Remove(key)
End Sub

Public Sub attachObserver(observer As AccountObserver, key As
        String)
    Call mvarObserverCollection.Add(observer, key)
End Sub


Private Sub Class_Initialize()
    Set mvarAccountEntryCollection = New Collection
    Set mvarObserverCollection = New Collection
End Sub

Private Sub Class_Terminate()
    Set mvarAccountEntryCollection = Nothing
    Set mvarObserverCollection = Nothing
End Sub
```

Account Entry

```
Option Explicit
Private mvarentryDate As Date
Private mvaramount As Currency
Public Property Let amount(ByVal vData As Currency)
    mvaramount = vData
End Property


Public Property Get amount() As Currency
    amount = mvaramount
End Property
```

```
Public Property Let entryDate(ByVal vData As Date)
    mvarentryDate = vData
End Property


Public Property Get entryDate() As Date
    entryDate = mvarentryDate
End Property
```

AccountObserver

```
Public Sub update(modifiedAccount As Account)
End Sub
```

Form Account Observer

```
Option Explicit
Implements AccountObserver

Dim mvarForm As Form

Public Sub setForm(theForm As Form)
    Set mvarForm = theForm
End Sub

Private Sub AccountObserver_update(modifiedAccount As Account)
    Call mvarForm.update(modifiedAccount)
End Sub
```

Java Observer

That wasn't too painful, but now let's consider the same approach in Java. In Java, there is direct language support for the observer. In order to provide a similar solution in Java, we simply implement the observer interface in the class that is to be notified. The *observable* class can be used to provide the framework for handling the registration and notification of observers. Notice how much more straightforward this is when the framework is in place. To avoid turning this example into a Java primer, I've avoided doing the GUI in Java (which, unfortunately, is something much more straightforward in Visual Basic than in Java).

Account

```
package JavaObserver;
import java.util.*;

public class Account extends Observable
```

```
    {

        public void addEntry(Date entryDate, double amount)
        {
            AccountEntry ae = new AccountEntry(entryDate, amount);
            m_entries.addElement(ae);
            setChanged();
        }

        public Enumeration getEntries()
        {
            return m_entries.elements();
        }

        private Vector m_entries;

    }
```

AccountEntry

```
package JavaObserver;
import java.util.Date;

public class AccountEntry
{
    AccountEntry(Date entryDate, double amount)
    {
        m_entryDate = entryDate;
        m_amount = amount;
    }

    public Date getEntryDate()
    {
        return m_entryDate;
    }

    public double getAmount()
    {
        return m_amount;
    }

    private Date m_entryDate;
    private double m_amount;
}
```

AccountObserver

```
package JavaObserver;
import java.util.*;
public class AccountObserver implements Observer
```

```
{
    public AccountObserver(Account account)
    {
        m_account = account;
        m_account.addObserver(this);
    }

    public void sync()
    {
        m_account.notifyObservers();
    }

    public void update(Observable observer, Object unused)
    {
        Account acct = (Account)observer;
        for(Enumeration e = acct.getEntries(); e.hasMoreElements();)
        {
            AccountEntry entry = (AccountEntry)e.nextElement();

            System.out.println(entry.getEntryDate().toString() +
    ":" + (new Double(entry.getAmount())).toString());
        }
    }
    private Account m_account;
}
```

Summary

In this chapter, we showed that even though programming languages can aid in the application of patterns by providing better support for certain idioms, patterns themselves transcend any specific language. This is not to underplay the importance of a programming language choice; it just recognizes that it should not limit our ability to provide valuable techniques.

Chapter

7

Patterns and System Development

When a person is faced with an act of design, what he does is governed
entirely by the pattern language which he has in his mind at that
moment. Of course, the pattern languages in each mind are evolving all
the time, as each person's experience grows. But at the particular
moment he has to make a design, he relies entirely on the pattern
language he happens to have accumulated up until that moment. His act
of design, whether humble or gigantically complex, is governed entirely
by the patterns he has in his mind at that moment, and his ability to
combine these patterns to form a new design.

—Alexander, 79

Building from Scratch

One of the places where patterns are most often applied is in developing a
new system. In designing a system architecture from the ground up, I take the
following approach:

- Understand your requirements

  Know what you don't know

  Know what's likely to change

- Create hinge points for the unknowns and entities that we suspect are likely to change
- Utilize supporting patterns to ensure no loose ends
- Make a sanity check
- Implement a little
- Restart the whole process at a lower level, as necessary

Now, let's create a fairly simple project to illustrate this approach:

Understanding Your Requirements

I know the following is obvious, but I am going to restate it here because it is so easily overlooked: Before you design a system or write any code or anything else, make sure you understand where you are going. Most problems are not coding or architectural problems but rather are requirements issues. Only by insuring that we understand not only the current but future requirements and direction, can we hope to design a successful product.

> Blackjack is a simple card game in which the player's goal is to get a better hand than the dealer without "busting" or going over 21 points. Aces count as 1 (in a soft hand) or 11; all face cards count as 10. The dealer must hit (draw another card) on all hands containing fewer than 17 points.
>
> We must create a text-based (console) computer simulation to allow us to try out different strategies prior to going to a real casino and losing real money. The purpose of this project is simply to simulate game play so betting support is not required. We must be able to automate a player strategy fully or play manually when developing this strategy. The code will be written in C++.

Know What You Don't Know

Look at those parts of the requirements that seem highly subject to change or are just not decided on yet. Those things that are decided on later in the requirements portion (usually the TBD items) are the most likely to change as you roll your product out to the customers. Each unknown can become a hinge point on which to allow the system to change. The first part of this activity is to abstract the unknown in such a way that we can define an interface that allows us to represent any of the possible solutions.

The following things are unknown at this phase so we will apply the first pattern discussed in this book, Pattern Name: High Road Development, in Chapter 1. Let's assume simple implementations for now, but in the next step we can create the ability to add more advanced capabilities later.

Blackjack has several variations; the standard approach requires the dealer to "stand" on soft 17. Because of a house advantage, several casinos have added a "hit" on the soft 17 option for the dealer. In addition, some casinos have also introduced a "double exposure" option, in which both cards are dealt to the dealer faceup (in exchange for reduced blackjack payouts, and the elimination of "pushes" or ties).

In addition, the strategy the player must use is unknown at this point, but we must be able to create new automated players by adding the new playing strategy and a single maintenance point.

Know What's Likely to Change

Several parts of your requirements may screen future release issues or are things that you are going to need to redo in the future. My way of handling these items is to recognize that if I choose a certain approach, it will probably be wrong. Instead, what I will do in this case is to abstract these areas of change again in such a way that we can define an interface that allows us to represent any of the possible solutions.

We know that the dealer's and player's strategies are likely to change because they are unknown. In addition, I almost always introduce IO as an unknown because the user interface is one of the most likely aspects in any system to change.

Create Hinge Points for the Unknowns and Entities that We Suspect Are Likely to Change

Every pattern provides some level of system variance. I believe this is the highest value, second to vocabulary, introduced in utilizing patterns. Once we have identified the places in which we have unknowns or areas likely to change and have some idea of what a proper abstraction or concept necessary to represent this variance is, we can simply utilize patterns to express them.

These areas now become hinge points, allowing us to connect new or different functionality.

In his book, *Multi-Paradigm Design for C++* [Cop, 99], Jim Coplien does a fantastic job of discussing commonality and variance and how they might be applied in developing a system. By applying analysis techniques (of which patterns play a part), we can more easily analyze a system or a domain, and we can more easily identify these hinge points.

> For the core framework (see Figure 7.1) we will first introduce the concepts of Deck and Cards. We will support multiple decks as well as single decks.

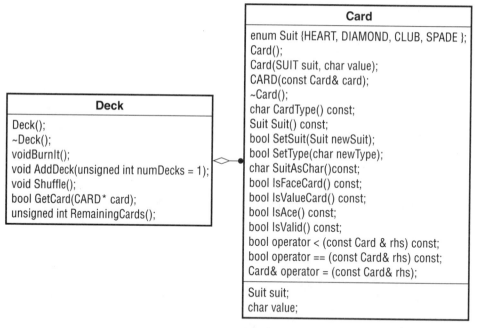

Figure 7.1   *Core framework*

> A Dealer class will be created to handle the implementation of the basic rules of the system. The interaction diagram is shown in Figure 7.2.

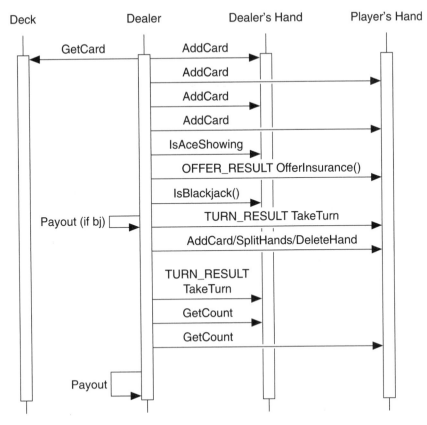

Figure 7.2 *Sequence diagram for play*

We will introduce a strategy pattern for the variation in the different types of player hands called BlackJackHand: Standard (PlayerHand, DealerHand, and SimulatedPlayerHand. A Strategy pattern [Gam, 95] allows us to vary the implementation of the specific algorithms used. Because much of the behavior in our strategies is the same right now, we will introduce a middle class called StandardBlackJackHand. As mentioned earlier, it is usually a good idea to introduce a common middle class to allow code to be reused. These middle classes can usually be refactored (or reorganized) into an existing design as needed, because there should never be any reference to them other than through their children. (See Figure 7.3 for the hand hierarchy.)

```
                      ┌─────────────────────────────────────────────────┐
                      │                 BlackJackHand                   │
                      ├─────────────────────────────────────────────────┤
                      │ enum TURN_RESULT { BUST, STAND, HIT, DOUBLE, SPLIT }; │
                      │ BlackJackHand(Displayer* displayer);            │
                      │ virtual ~BlackJackHand();                       │
                      │ virtual unsigned int LowCount() const;          │
                      │ virtual unsigned int HighCount() const;         │
                      │ virtual bool IsBlackJack() const;               │
                      │ virtual void AddCard(const Card& card);         │
                      │ virtual unsigned int NumCards();                │
                      │ virtual const CARD& GetCard(unsigned int which); │
                      │ virtual void Reset();                           │
                      │ virtual bool TookInsurance(){ return false; }   │
                      │ virtual bool OfferInsurance(){ return false; }  │
                      │ virtual TURN_RESULT TakeTurn() = 0;             │
                      │ virtual bool IsAceShowing() const;              │
                      │ virtual const char* GetIdentifier() const;      │
                      └─────────────────────────────────────────────────┘
```

```
                      ┌─────────────────────────────────────────────────┐
                      │              StandardBlackJackHand              │
                      ├─────────────────────────────────────────────────┤
                      │ StandardBlackJackHand(Displayer* displayer);    │
                      │ unsigned int LowCount() const;                  │
                      │ unsigned int HighCount() const;                 │
                      │ bool IsBlackJack() const;                       │
                      │ void AddCard(const Card& card);                 │
                      │ unsigned int NumCards();                        │
                      │ const CARD& GetCard(unsigned int which);        │
                      │ void Reset();                                   │
                      │ virtual bool TookInsurance() { return false; }  │
                      │ virtual bool OfferInsurance() { return false; } │
                      │ virtual TURN_RESULT TakeTurn() = 0;             │
                      │ bool IsAceShowing() const;                      │
                      │ Displayer* GetDisplayer();                      │
                      │ const char* GetIdentifier() const;              │
                      └─────────────────────────────────────────────────┘
```

```
┌──────────────────────────────┐ ┌──────────────────────────────┐ ┌──────────────────────────────┐
│          DealerHand          │ │          PlayerHand          │ │      SimulatedPlayerHand     │
├──────────────────────────────┤ ├──────────────────────────────┤ ├──────────────────────────────┤
│ TURN_RESULT TakeTurn();      │ │ TURN_RESULT TakeTurn();      │ │ TURN_RESULT TakeTurn();      │
│ const char* GetIdentifier() const; │ │ bool TookInsurance();    │ │ bool TookInsurance();        │
│                              │ │ bool OfferInsurance();       │ │ bool OfferInsurance();       │
│                              │ │ const char* GetIdentifier() const; │ │ const char* GetIdentifier() const; │
└──────────────────────────────┘ └──────────────────────────────┘ └──────────────────────────────┘
```

Figure 7.3 *The hand hierarchy*

We will also decouple ourselves from the display rules by creating a Displayer interface (see Figure 7.4) that handles all display rules. For now we will implement only a Standard Displayer that handles the console text-based rules.

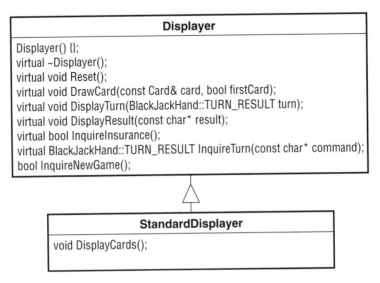

Displayer
Displayer() {};
virtual ~Displayer();
virtual void Reset();
virtual void DrawCard(const Card& card, bool firstCard);
virtual void DisplayTurn(BlackJackHand::TURN_RESULT turn);
virtual void DisplayResult(const char* result);
virtual bool InquireInsurance();
virtual BlackJackHand::TURN_RESULT InquireTurn(const char* command);
bool InquireNewGame();

StandardDisplayer
void DisplayCards();

Figure 7.4 *Displayer hierarchy*

Utilize Supporting Patterns to Ensure No Loose Ends

Once we have the patterns in place to provide us this system variance, we need to connect it to the overall architecture. Usually this involves adding structural or creational patterns to the fledgling architecture. It is essential to ensure that when new or different functionality is to be added to the system, only one point in the existing system is ever changed. This is the point at which we decide to use the new functionality; usually this involves making sure that any creational patterns to decouple the implementation classes are in place. This is not to imply that patterns can simply be "plugged in"; instead the problem (and the context) must be well understood to ensure the proper application.

> Let's look at the high level of our system at this point (see Figure 7.5). I might consider adding a creation pattern such as a Factory Method pattern [Gam, 95] to isolate the creation of the different types of blackjack hands. However, an examination of the architecture at this point shows only a single point that references the concrete classes, and I can add the creational support later without any advantage. Because there is no advantage to adding it now and we can always add it later, let's leave it as is for now.

Make a Sanity Check

Now, examine the architecture and ensure that we have sufficient flexibility. While the architecture may not be easy, especially for the more ambitious designer, one must also make sure it is not overly complex for the designated implementers. It is extremely painful to design a beautiful and elegant framework only to have to go back and revisit it because it cannot be implemented by the coders. This occurs when we fail to consider the audience of the patterns and we fail to understand design complexity vs. code complexity. A simpler design often leads to more (and often more complex) code—but not always. However, many developers can understand complex code more than they can think in terms of abstraction, so training is essential to get over this curve. This is especially true with novice developers who have little experience in enterprise systems or who are used to working in an environment that is more code-feedback-intensive, such as Web design.

> The architecture, as it stands now, is fairly straightforward, and C++, the language in which we implement this, easily supports all of the design mechanisms we are using. Therefore we can freely continue into implementation.

Implement a Little

Now comes the easy part—coding. The choice of programming languages is an important one, but it is more often a question of existing skill levels than of the specific language itself. Unfortunately, language choices (and operating systems) are often more of a religious debate than a technical one. The key, in my opinion, is always to look at a programming language as a tool, and it

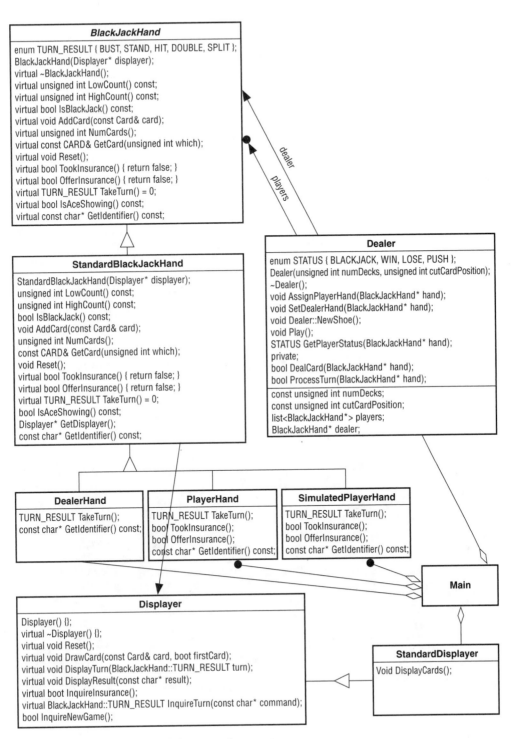

Figure 7.5 *A high-level diagram of our system*

becomes simply a question of what is the "right" tool for the job. Realize that any programming language carries with it certain things (forces) that it does well and certain things (forces) it does not do well. If your architecture relies on multiple-inheritance techniques and the language choice is Visual Basic (which supports only a single-inheritance model), then we must change either the architecture or the language used. Sometimes we have to do both.

Implement a small part of your system to prove that the underlying architecture and approach are sound.

> Some important things to consider in implementing this architecture is that we first should define the core interfaces for BlackJackHand and Displayer. From that point forward we can place multiple developers on the subclasses and on other parts of the system. This gives us amazing freedom in allowing parallel development of this system. As you can see in Figure 7.6, the code itself is actually fairly simple, or at least as simple as a trivial single module approach would be. In addition, it should be obvious that the testing of each unit by the developer can be done quickly, and this system may evolve at a rapid pace.

See Appendix C: Blackjack Code for detail code.

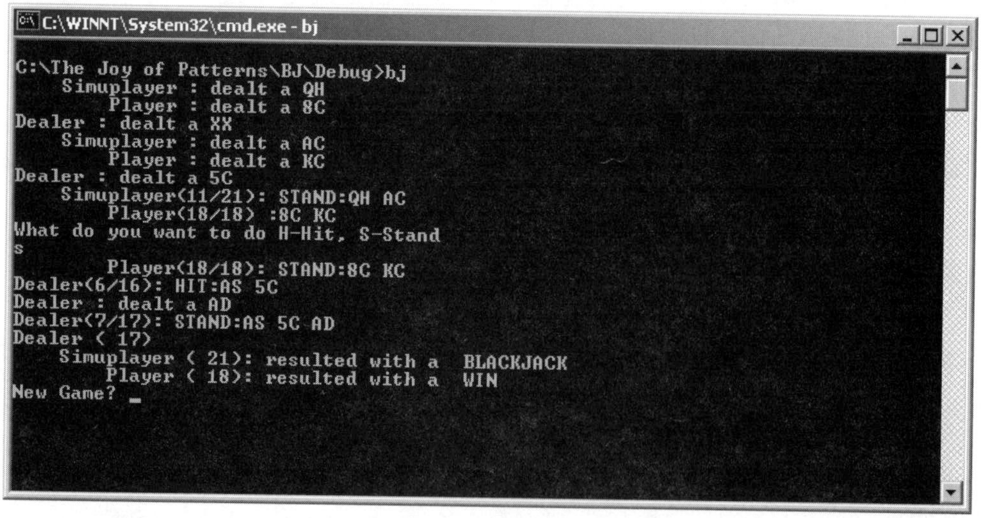

Figure 7.6 *Sample program execution*

Restart the Whole Process at a Lower Level, as Necessary

Now we should have a small portion of the system built forming a core of our system. In all but the most trivial systems, we must now begin the entire process again. The difference is that this cycle is now constrained by the existing application. As we go through each iteration, the system becomes more constrained, much like an empty house we are trying to furnish. As you continue to furnish it, the amount of room left, as well as the choices available to match the remaining pieces, becomes less and less. Luckily, I am far better at software development than interior decoration.

The one major change I might introduce to this project at this point is to abstract the dealer another layer. This would allow the exact rules to vary without a code change. I asked myself if there was any advantage to doing this now as opposed to later, and I decided to postpone it until necessary.

A useful exercise is to add a logging mechanism to record all game play for review. This can be done by adding a Decorator (see the previous Burger example for more information on the decorator), as follows:

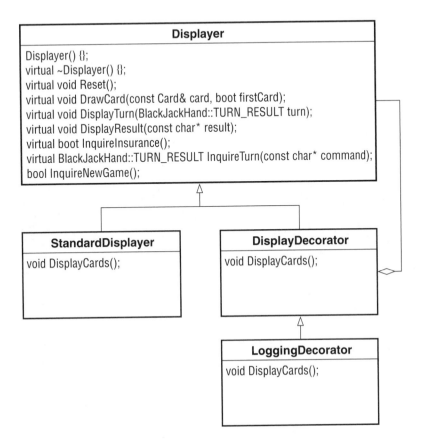

Summary

This chapter provides an end-to-end definition and implementation of a small blackjack game system. Because of the separation of concerns between the display, game play, and card framework, we can easily support multiple developers and have a relatively high degree of parallel development (especially for a toy example). In addition, it should become apparent to the reader that this system is relatively easy to test and to extend. Because multiple iterations of developing this system are possible, we can keep our design cycles in short periods of time, which more easily keeps our projects on target.

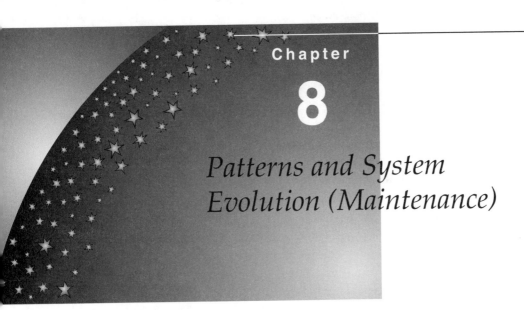

Patterns and System Evolution (Maintenance)

[Elegance is]. . . that elusive quality of coolness that every programmer admires and strives for, yet cannot name. Elegant software is simple. Elegant software is clever, yet not obscure. Elegant software solves complex problems through wonderfully inventive mechanisms that are semantically rich enough to be applied to other, perhaps totally unrelated problems. Elegance means finding just the right abstraction. Elegance means using limited resources in novel ways.

—Booch, 96

Maintenance

Most software development work is not done by developing new systems. The majority of work is done in existing systems involving either changing or adding functionality. This form of evolutionary development is often called "maintenance," although the division between development and maintenance is an arbitrary one. In fact, if you are using an iterative development approach such as that recommended throughout this book, there really is no division. The distinction that does exist, however, is that you have existing internal or external customers. The problem is that modifying existing "working" code often increases its complexity, making it more brittle and much harder to maintain. In addition, most approaches to maintenance violate the Open-Closed Principle discussed earlier. We often require a developer to understand fully the existing code in addition to the new functionality. This often results in breaking code that worked. While a hacking approach to development, where you go in, change code, quickly test, and then ship, may work in the short term, in the long term it causes the system to collapse onto its own mass as the complexity and maintenance costs rise and eventually no longer justify keeping the system.

If you have a well-developed system, such as the type this book tries to encourage, then adding or changing the system should be relatively straight-forward, and this maintenance complexity can be kept down much longer. However, no matter how much you think ahead and try to read the future, you will miss something. This will require you to add something new. Besides, if you added *everything* to your system up front, the system would quickly become too large and complex to maintain, and you would never ship anything. By the way, contrary to many approaches, the bottom line in all software development efforts is actually to get working code in the hands of the end user as quickly as possible. This brings us back to the earlier principle: Keep your system as open as possible architecturally, but do not code (or otherwise pay for) any part of the system you don't need now.

Most maintenance effort is concerned with adding new behavior or modifying existing behavior of a system. Obviously you must first define this new behavior in terms of your existing system. Once that is done you must consider the impact of this change. Specifically, do you provide a mechanism to allow the system to vary to add this behavior? Let's think again about a system as containing extension or "hinge" points in which to allow an aspect of the system to vary. Patterns provide a large amount of support for system variance. Looking at the 23 GOF patterns that follow in Table 8.1, for example, we see the areas of variance provided by them.

The key to making any change is to follow three basic steps:

1. **Understand the new behavior and the impact of change.**

   In understanding the new behavior and analyzing the impact of this change, patterns are invaluable. If you have documented your system appropriately, you will have a very high-level schematic of sorts to understand how your system works, making it much easier to determine what impact these changes will have. In addition, it becomes easier to see the "hinge" points where expansion can be easily accomplished.

Table 8.1   *GOF Pattern and Their Variances [Gam, 95]*

Pattern	Varies
Creational	
Abstract Factory	Specific set of objects that can be created
Builder	Rules of assembling a complex object
Factory Method	Specific kind that is created
Prototype	Class of object and its associated data
Singleton	The sole instance of a class
Structural	
Adapter	Interface
Bridge	Implementation
Composite	Composition or building up of functionality
Decorator	Responsibilities
Facade	Interface to a subsystem
Flyweight	Storage Costs
Proxy	Location or access to an object
Behavioral	
Chain of Responsibility	Who serves a request for an object
Command	When and how a request is handled
Interpreter	Grammar of a language
Iterator	Traversal of an aggregate object
Mediator	How and which objects communicate
Memento	External storage of private data
Observer	Number of objects dependent on a source of information and synchronization methods
State	Set of states or modes
Strategy	Family of algorithm
Template Method	Steps of an algorithm
Visitor	Operations on a class

2. Add or change the behavior by

a. an existing pattern in place.

If a hinge point or pattern already exists in the system, it is simply a matter of using it and providing the simple point of change to take advantage of the new functionality. Normally this is done by creating new implementation classes, and the new point of change will be in the Creational Pattern used to hide/select the implementation class.

b. adding a new pattern that provides the framework in which to add the new/changed functionality behavior.

If, however, the hinge point doesn't already exist in the system, then we must add one without breaking the system. The key is to determine the appropriate changes you need to make to the system to add this new functionality in the simplest manner possible. Patterns provide a target for where we want the system to go, but they don't really tell us how to move from Step 1 to Step n. The answer is through refactoring. Refactoring is reorganizing a program so that the core functionality remains unchanged but the code is able to take advantage of extensions. It should be obvious that in order to do refactoring successfully you must guarantee that the behavior does not change. To accomplish this goal, you must have comprehensive regression test suites. Refactoring is a relatively new topic in software development. Most of the recent interest began with the Ph.D. thesis of William Opdyke [Opd, 92]. Martin Fowler [Fow, 99] does an excellent job of giving a step-by-step description of how to proceed with each of the identified refactorings he discusses and a step-by-step approach of how to apply certain refactorings. This approach will help pinpoint the place in the existing system that has the core functionality. There is also a fair amount of research (especially among the SmallTalk community) to automate this refactoring. This would allow a safer approach because productivity can increase and human error can decrease if we can automate these steps. These tools are still in their infancy though and, like many case tools in the past, may not emerge to fruition.

c. standard design and coding.

Never forget that our goal is the successful implementation of a software system, not simply the creation of an elaborate design. While the excitement over learning new tools is often overpowering, we must not lose sight of our goals and forget to apply standard design and coding practices where appropriate. Again, let simplicity be a strong force in your evaluation of solutions (along with extensibility, testability, and the elegance of design).

3. Test and deploy.

If we have done everything right, the testing and deployment should be relatively straightforward. In fact, each new functionality we add to our system should impact only a single point in the system (the point at which we decide to use the new functionary) or a single area in which we refactored the design to add this capability. In fact, I have found that most changes can even be made without significant recompilation. My thinking is that if you didn't need to recompile an area of code, you probably didn't break it. This is not to imply that testing is easy but rather that patterns may make this hard problem a little easier.

A Quick Example

Let's take a simple example: Say we want to start allowing complex pricing to be used for objects in our earlier Product Configuration example (see page 45). Specifically, I would like to support three pricing alternatives: a fixed price, a price computed by summing the subparts, and a real-time price that consults an external database for the price. If you recall, our final high-level solution looked liked that in Figure 8.1.

It should be fairly straightforward to understand that the pricing calculation needs to affect only the part hierarchy. But how do we provide a way in which to allow the flexibility for pricing that we envision is necessary? When we look at the existing patterns we want to use, the questions that arise are is the price an algorithm used by a part, or can a part have one of many pricing states? This will help decide if a Strategy pattern or State pattern [Gam, 95] is more appropriate. We looked at the State pattern earlier (see State on page 50); the Strategy pattern is similar.

Strategy Pattern

Intent

Define a family of algorithms, encapsulate each one, and make them interchangeable. Strategy lets the algorithm vary independently from clients that use it.

Varies

Varies includes an algorithm or a family of algorithms.

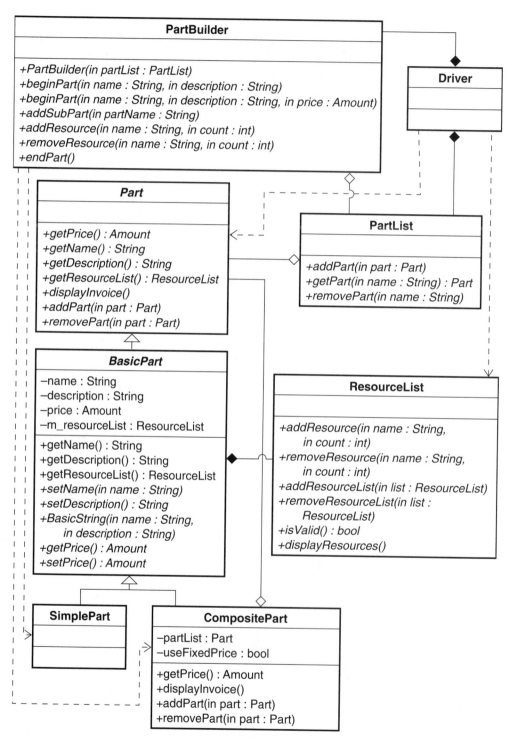

Figure 8.1 *Product Configuration example*

Structure

Figure 8.2 illustrates the Strategy structure.

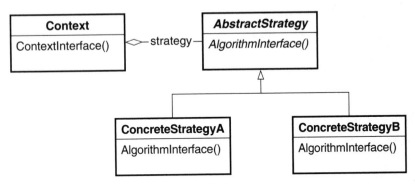

Figure 8.2 *Strategy structure*

Comments

This pattern is very similar to the State pattern in structure, but conceptually both have a very different intent. The key determination of whether behavior is driven by the state or the set of algorithms may seem arbitrary, but it needs to be considered. Normally, State is internal to the object, and strategies can be external, but this is not a hard and fast rule.

I have found it useful to implement a Strategy pattern for common error handling capability in products. Often when a project is divided among multiple developers, different mechanisms for displaying errors evolve. This can make things very difficult later when the various parts are integrated, by providing a common interface such as

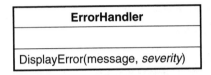

This error Handler can be requested from a factory method when it is required or passed to the appropriate routines at construction.

Then at run time we can provide different mechanisms such as a windows-based mechanism using MsgBox, a console-based display using text output, a file-based mechanism, or even SNMP alerts that tools can use to detect these problems. Any combination of these mechanisms can be chosen (at run time as well) without impacting any of the code already in place. By deciding on the use of the errorHandling interface up front, we can postpone the final decisions as well.

Either of these two patterns can be successfully applied in this situation. We need to weigh the trade-offs. In my experience, part of this determination is whether the pricing rules exist outside of the part (in which case a Strategy pattern is more appropriate) or inside of the part (in which case a State pattern is more appropriate). Based on the decision of the earlier view to have a fixed or composite price be a mode of the CompositePart, I will use a State pattern for consistency. I will make the state objects lightweight by passing the part information as a external variable on the calculation so that they can be shared. A Flyweight pattern [Gam, 95] that would allow sharing of light-weight objects can be used here, but because the object is now totally stateless, we do not receive any real benefit by introducing object pooling. Figure 8.3 illustrates the new pricing mode.

In order to make the selection of Pricing mode completely dynamic, we add a selection method to Part. As always, we avoid storing any data members in the interface or abstract class and put the storage into the intermediary class BasicPart. Now we can remove the flag and getPrice() routine used at the CompositePart because the BasicPart object can now fully handle this calculation. Figure 8.4 shows the updated pricing framework.

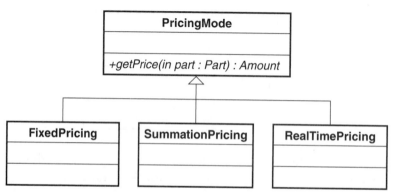

Figure 8.3 *The new pricing mode*

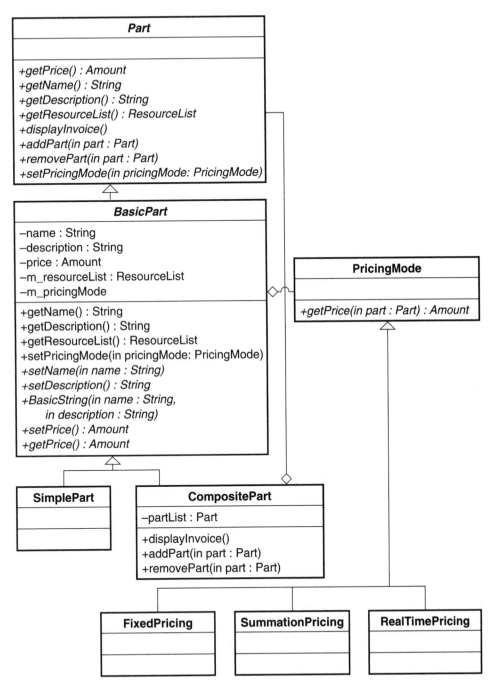

Figure 8.4 *The updated pricing framework*

PartBuilder
+PartBuilder(in partList : PartList) +beginPart(in name : String, in description : String) +beginPart(in name : String, in description : String, in price : Amount) +addSubPart(in partName : String) +addResource(in name : String, in count : int) +removeResource(in name : String, in count : int) +endPart +setPricingMode(in mode : String)

Figure 8.5 *The updated PartBuilder*

The only remaining area where we need to modify the system is the point at which the decision to use the appropriate pricing mode is made, the builder. We can add a simple PricingMode selection capability here and make the builder responsible for creating the appropriate pricing class. This means that additional pricing modes can be added, and the only point of impact going forward will be the builder. In effect, we have now fully provided the hinge points for infinite pricing variances. Figure 8.5 illustrates the updated part builder.

Our extended system is illustrated in Figure 8.6.

Note that we can now put many parallel teams to work implementing the different pricing modes as well as each part of our system. In addition, it should be easy to see that by adding this functionality the code complexity has not been increased (although design complexity has). In fact, it could be argued that this is even a simpler system to code and test after this reorganization.

Summary

Maintenance is evolving a system that is already seeing the benefit of being used. By using patterns and applying reorganization of code through refactoring, it is possible to continue to keep a system from becoming overly complex through maintenance and, in fact, continually to improve the ability to extend the system. This eliminates the view of maintenance as the dreaded nightmare of software, causing us to understand that it is part of the normal product life cycle and evolution.

Figure 8.6 *The product configuration system with pricing modes*

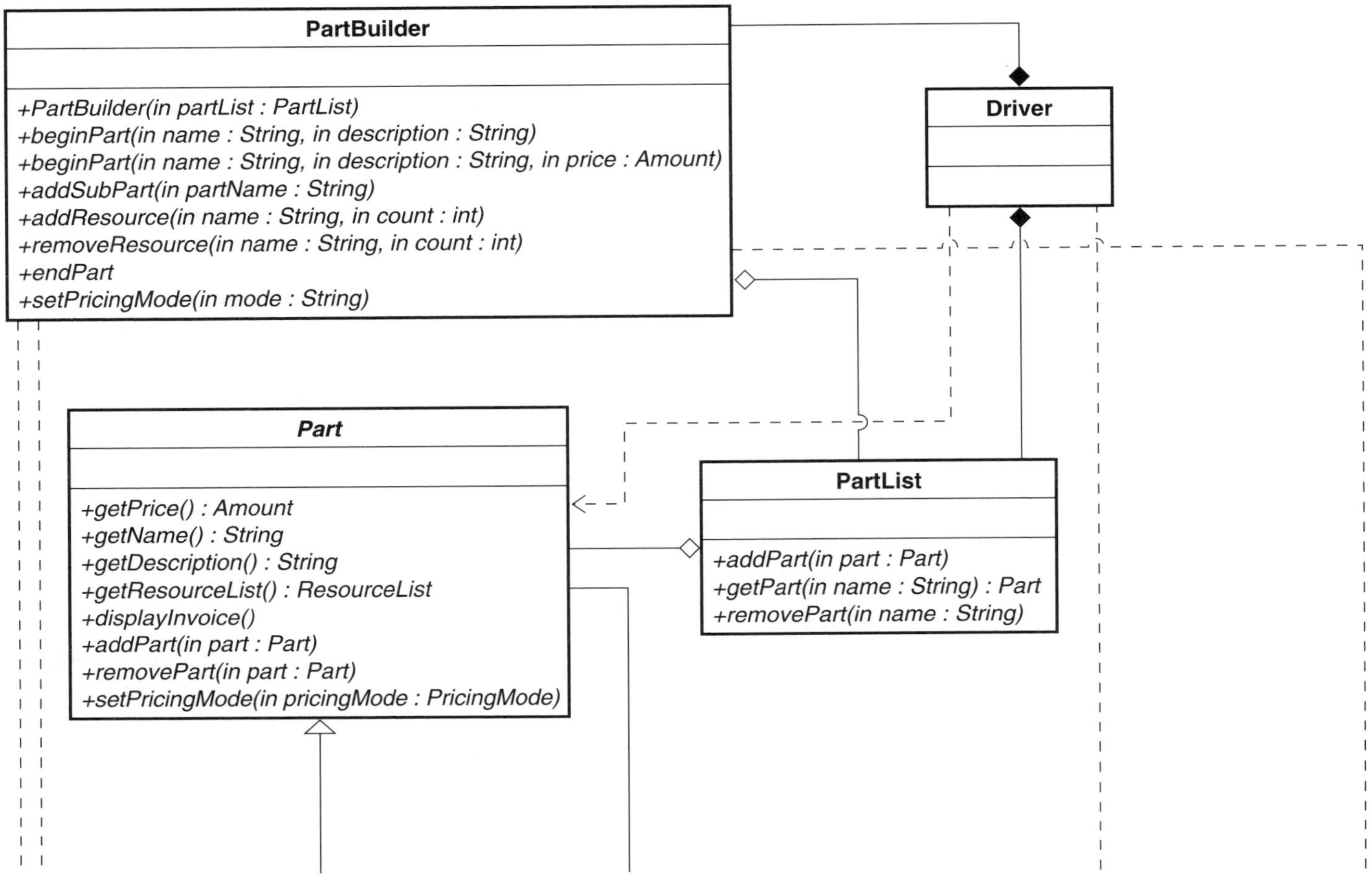

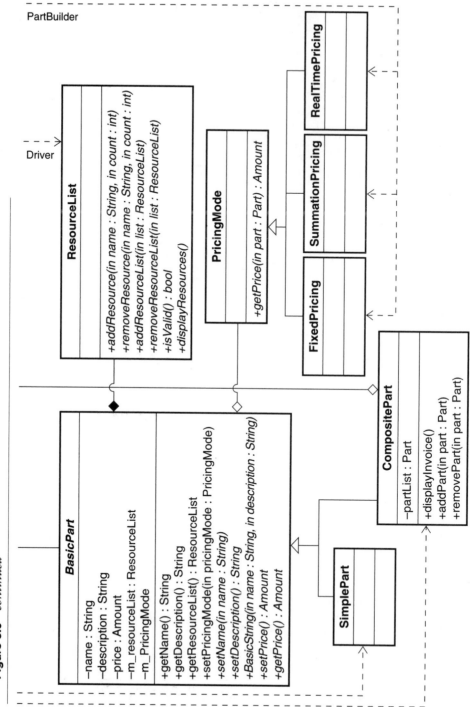

Figure 8.6 *continued*

Closing Thoughts

The most important thing is that you take the
pattern seriously. There is no point at all in using
the pattern if you only give lip service to it.

—*Alexander, 79*

In this book we reviewed the basics of software development and object-oriented development. We also covered the core concepts that comprise patterns, explaining context and form and the role forces play in understanding the appropriateness of using patterns. Through a series of design examples, we could see some of the various places that patterns enter the software development activity and the benefit they add there.

Hopefully, by combining the examples and methods of applying patterns in both initial system design and maintenance, you feel ready to go out and take advantage of this exciting area. However, I caution you to focus on the basics, consider the context at work before applying a pattern. As shown in several examples, sometimes applying a pattern where the context does not warrant it, serves only to make things more complex to build. It is extremely difficult at times to balance the elegance of design with raw simplicity to get the job done (and then continual refactoring of the architecture as the program evolves).

At this point, I recommend that you delve deeper into patterns and read some of the references at the end of the book. I also recommend that you consider using the pattern form to document your reusable design solutions. It focuses you to think about the rationale of your solutions and gives you, as a developer, a better insight into why something was good and how it could be better. I've found that putting a design idea into pattern form sometimes leads me to think about the problem in new and exciting ways.

Well, that's it in a nutshell (oops, different series). Hopefully, this book has inspired you to look at the process of developing software in a new and exciting way. It is my sincere hope that the paradigm shift I've observed in teaching patterns and consulting has occurred for you reading this book. In either case, I appreciate any feedback or experiences you may have, so please feel free to write to me at the following e-mail address: brandon@goldfedder.com.

A

Product Code

Part.java

```java
package ProductConfig;
import java.io.PrintStream;

class NotACompositeException extends Exception {
    NotACompositeException() { super(); }
    NotACompositeException(String s) { super(s); }
}

public abstract class Part
{

public abstract double getPrice();

public abstract String getName();

public abstract String getDescription();

public abstract ResourceList getResourceList();

public abstract void displayInvoice(PrintStream stream, int level);

public abstract void addPart(Part part) throws
    NotACompositeException;

public abstract void removePart(Part part) throws
    NotACompositeException;;
}
```

BasicPart.java

```java
package ProductConfig;
import java.io.PrintStream;

public abstract class BasicPart extends Part
{

BasicPart(String name, String description, double price)
{
        m_name = name;
        m_description = description;
        m_price = price;
        m_resourceList = new ResourceList();
}

public void setName(String name)
{
    m_name = name;
}

public void setDescription(String description)
{
    m_description = description;
}

public String getName()
{
    return m_name;
}

public String getDescription()
{
    return m_description;
}

public double getPrice()
{
    return m_price;
}

public void setPrice(double price)
{
    price = m_price;
}

public void displayInvoice(PrintStream str, int level)
{
    for (int i = 0; i < level; ++i)
```

```
    {
        str.print(" ");
    }

    str.println(this.toString());
}

public String toString()
{
    return m_name + ":" + m_description + ":" +
            Double.toString(getPrice());
}

public ResourceList getResourceList()
{
    return m_resourceList;
}

private ResourceList m_resourceList;
private String m_name;
private String m_description;
private double m_price;

}
```

SimplePart.java

```
package ProductConfig;
import java.util.Vector;
public class SimplePart extends BasicPart
{
SimplePart(String name, String description, double price)
{
    super(name, description, price);
}

public void addPart(Part part) throws NotACompositeException
{
    throw new NotACompositeException();
}

public void removePart(Part part) throws NotACompositeException
{
    throw new NotACompositeException();
}

}
```

CompositePart.java

```java
package ProductConfig;
import java.io.PrintStream;
import java.util.*;

public class CompositePart extends BasicPart
{
// use a fixed algorithm for price
CompositePart(String name, String description, double price)
{
    super(name, description, price);
    m_useFixed = true;
    m_parts = new Vector();
}

// Use a calculated algorigthm for price
CompositePart(String name, String description)
{
    super(name, description, 0);
    m_useFixed = false;
    m_parts = new Vector();
}

private double sumChildrenPrices()
{
    double price = 0;
    for (Enumeration e = m_parts.elements() ;
      e.hasMoreElements() ; )
    {
        Part tmpPart = (Part)e.nextElement();
        price = price + tmpPart.getPrice();
    }
    return price;
}

public void addPart(Part part) throws NotACompositeException
{
    getResourceList().addResourceList(part.getResourceList());
    m_parts.addElement(part);
}

public void removePart(Part part) throws NotACompositeException
{
    getResourceList().removeResourceList(part.getResourceList());
    m_parts.removeElement(part);
}
```

```
public double getPrice()
{
// If we are using fixed then get the Parent
//base price, otherwise sum the children prices
    return  (m_useFixed) ? super.getPrice() :
            sumChildrenPrices();
}

public void displayInvoice(PrintStream str, int level)
{
    final int LEVEL_INCREMENT = 5;
    super.displayInvoice(str, level);

    for (Enumeration e = m_parts.elements() ;
      e.hasMoreElements() ; )
    {
        Part tmpPart = (Part)e.nextElement();
        tmpPart.displayInvoice(str, level +
            LEVEL_INCREMENT);
    }
}

private Vector m_parts;
private boolean m_useFixed;

}
```

PartList.java

```
package ProductConfig;
import java.util.*;
public class PartList
{
public PartList()
{
    m_partList = new Hashtable();
}

public Part getPart(String name)
{
    return (Part)(m_partList.get(name));
}

public void addPart(Part part)
{
    m_partList.put(part.getName(),part);
}
```

```java
    public void removePart(Part part)
    {
        m_partList.remove(part.getName());
    }


    private Hashtable m_partList;
}
```

ResourceList.java

```java
package ProductConfig;
import java.util.*;
import java.io.PrintStream;

public class ResourceList
{
public ResourceList()
{
    m_resList = new Hashtable();
}

public void addResource(String name, int count)
{
    Integer resourceCount = (Integer)m_resList.get(name);
    if (resourceCount != null)
    {
        m_resList.remove(name);
        m_resList.put(name, new Integer
        (resourceCount.intValue() + count) );
    }
    else
    {
        m_resList.put(name,new Integer(count));
    }
}


public void removeResource(String name, int count)
{
    addResource(name, - count);
}

// Check if the resource configuration is valid
public boolean isValid()
{
    boolean flag = true;
    for (Enumeration e = m_resList.elements() ; flag &&
        e.hasMoreElements() ; )
    {
        Integer resourceCount = (Integer)e.nextElement();
```

```
              flag  = flag & (resourceCount.intValue() >= 0);
       }
       return flag;
}

public void addResourceList(ResourceList newList1)
{
    //  Loop through the keys
    for (Enumeration e = newList1.m_resList.keys() ;
      e.hasMoreElements() ; )
    {
        String keyName = (String)e.nextElement();
        addResource(keyName,
        ((Integer)newList1.m_resList.get(keyName)).intValue());
    }
}

public void removeResourceList(ResourceList newList1)
{
    // Loop through the keys
    for (Enumeration e = newList1.m_resList.keys() ;
      e.hasMoreElements() ; )
    {
        String keyName = (String)e.nextElement();
        removeResource(keyName,
        ((Integer)newList1.m_resList.get(keyName)).intValue());
    }
}

public String toString()
{
    return Integer.toString(m_resList.size()) +
        " Elements.";
}

public void displayResources(PrintStream str)
{
    for (Enumeration e = m_resList.keys() ; e.hasMoreElements() ; )
    {
        String keyName = (String)e.nextElement();
        Integer count =  (Integer)m_resList.get(keyName);
        str.println(keyName + " : " + count.toString());
    }
}

private Hashtable m_resList;

}
```

Driver.java

```
package ProductConfig;

public class Driver
{

// Put some stuff in the part list
public static void fillPartList(PartList list)
{
Part newPart = new SimplePart("Aplo2", "Apollo 2 Motherboard",109);
  // provides PCI slots+
  newPart.getResourceList().addResource("PCI Slots",5);
  newPart.getResourceList().addResource("DIMM",3);
  newPart.getResourceList().addResource("AGP Port",1);
  newPart.getResourceList().addResource("Slot 1",1);
  // consumes a motherboard
  newPart.getResourceList().removeResource("Motherboard",1);
list.addPart(newPart);

newPart = new SimplePart("Sota24", "Sota 24",115);
  // provides PCI slots+
  newPart.getResourceList().addResource("PCI Slots",5);
  newPart.getResourceList().addResource("DIMM",3);
  newPart.getResourceList().addResource("Slot 1",1);
  // consumes a motherboard
  newPart.getResourceList().removeResource("Motherboard",1);
list.addPart(newPart);

newPart = new SimplePart("MX24","Std Mid-sized Tower Case",59);
  newPart.getResourceList().addResource("Motherboard",1);
list.addPart(newPart);


newPart = new SimplePart("FX24","Std Full-sized Tower Case",79);
  newPart.getResourceList().addResource("Motherboard",1);
list.addPart(newPart);

newPart = new SimplePart("I550","550Mhz Slot 1 Processor",300);
  newPart.getResourceList().removeResource("Slot 1",1);
list.addPart(newPart);

newPart = new SimplePart("I600","600Mhz Slot 1 Processor",350);
  newPart.getResourceList().removeResource("Slot 1",1);
list.addPart(newPart);

newPart = new SimplePart("D128","128MB Dimm Memory",120);
  newPart.getResourceList().removeResource("DIMM",1);
list.addPart(newPart);
```

```
newPart = new SimplePart("D256","256MB Dimm Memory - 1 slot",270);
  newPart.getResourceList().removeResource("DIMM",1);
list.addPart(newPart);

newPart = new SimplePart("D256-2","256MB Dimm Memory - 2
    slots",230);
  newPart.getResourceList().removeResource("DIMM",2);
list.addPart(newPart);

newPart = new CompositePart("BBC1","BareBones Config 1",300);
  newPart.addPart(list.getPart("Sota24"));
  newPart.addPart(list.getPart("I550"));
  newPart.addPart(list.getPart("MX24"));
list.addPart(newPart);

}
/**
 * Test Driver Main - Creates a simple configuration and outputs it.
 *
 */
public static void main (String[] args)
{
    PartList list = new PartList();
    fillPartList(list);
    Part base = new CompositePart("Galaxy Pro 200","Basic
    setup system");
    base.addPart(list.getPart("BBC1"));
    base.addPart(list.getPart("D256"));
    base.displayInvoice(System.out, 0);
    System.out.println("Resource are: " +
    (base.getResourceList().isValid() ? "Valid" : "Invalid"));
    base.getResourceList().displayResources(System.out);
}
}
```

The program results in the following output:

```
Galaxy Pro 200:Basic setup system:570.0
    BBC1:BareBones Config 1:300.0
        Sota24:Sota 24:115.0
        I550:550Mhz Slot 1 Processor:300.0
        MX24:Std Mid-sized Tower Case:59.0
    D256:256MB Dimm Memory - 1 slot:270.0
Resource are: Valid
Motherboard: 0
DIMM: 2
Slot 1: 0
PCI Slots: 5
```

Additonal Code

PartBuilder.java

```java
package ProductConfig;
public class PartBuilder
{
public PartBuilder(PartList partList)
{
    m_partList = partList;
}

public void beginPart(String name , String description )
{
    // We will use a composite part as the holding queue
    // if it turns out to be simple we will simply
    // transform it later
    m_pendingPart = new CompositePart(name,description);
    m_isComposite = false;
}

public void beginPart(String name , String description ,
double price)
{
    // We will use a composite part as the holding queue
    // if it turns out to be simple we will simply
    // transform it later
    m_pendingPart = new CompositePart(name,description,price);
    m_isComposite = false;
}

public void endPart()
{
    // if it's not composite transform it
    if (!m_isComposite)
    {
    String name = m_pendingPart.getName();
    String description = m_pendingPart.getDescription();
    double price = m_pendingPart.getPrice();
    ResourceList rList = m_pendingPart.getResourceList();
    m_pendingPart = new SimplePart(name, description, price);
    m_pendingPart.getResourceList().addResourceList(rList);
    }

    m_partList.addPart(m_pendingPart);
    // After adding it invalidate it from memory
    m_pendingPart = null;
}

public void addSubPart(String name)
```

```
{
    try
    {
       m_isComposite = true;
       m_pendingPart.addPart(m_partList.getPart(name));
    }
    catch (Exception NotACompositeException)
    {
       m_isComposite = false;
       // TBD: Recovery kept simple for now: just ignore
    }
}

public void addResource(String name, int count)
{
    m_pendingPart.getResourceList().addResource(name, count);
}

public void removeResource(String name, int count)
{
    m_pendingPart.getResourceList().removeResource(name, count);
}


    private PartList m_partList;
    private boolean m_isComposite;
    private Part m_pendingPart;
}
```

new driver.java

```
/**
 * This class can take a variable number of parameters on the
       command
 * line. Program execution begins with the main() method. The class
 * constructor is not invoked unless an object of type 'Class1'
 * created in the main() method.
 */
package ProductConfig;
public class Driver
{

public static void fillPartList(PartBuilder builder)
{
    builder.beginPart("Aplo2", "Apollo 2 Motherboard",109);
        builder.addResource("PCI Slots",5);
        builder.addResource("DIMM",3);
        builder.addResource("AGP Port",1);
        builder.addResource("Slot 1",1);
        builder.removeResource("Motherboard",1);
    builder.endPart();
```

```
        builder.beginPart("Sota24", "Sota 24",115);
            builder.addResource("PCI Slots",5);
            builder.addResource("DIMM",3);
            builder.addResource("Slot 1",1);
            builder.removeResource("Motherboard",1);
        builder.endPart();

        builder.beginPart("MX24","Std Mid-sized Tower Case",59);
            builder.addResource("Motherboard",1);
        builder.endPart();


        builder.beginPart("FX24","Std Full-sized Tower Case",79);
            builder.addResource("Motherboard",1);
        builder.endPart();

        builder.beginPart("I550","550Mhz Slot 1 Processor",300);
            builder.removeResource("Slot 1",1);
        builder.endPart();

        builder.beginPart("I600","600Mhz Slot 1 Processor",350);
            builder.removeResource("Slot 1",1);
        builder.endPart();

        builder.beginPart("D128","128MB Dimm Memory",120);
            builder.removeResource("DIMM",1);
        builder.endPart();

        builder.beginPart("D256","256MB Dimm Memory - 1 slot",270);
            builder.removeResource("DIMM",1);
        builder.endPart();

        builder.beginPart("D256-2","256MB Dimm Memory - 2 slots",230);
            builder.removeResource("DIMM",2);
        builder.endPart();

        builder.beginPart("BBC1","BareBones Config 1",300);
            builder.addSubPart("Sota24");
            builder.addSubPart("I550");
            builder.addSubPart("MX24");
        builder.endPart();

    }

    public static void main (String[] args)
    {
        PartList list = new PartList();
        PartBuilder builder = new PartBuilder(list);

        fillPartList(builder);
```

```
      builder.beginPart("Galaxy Pro 200","Basic setup system");
          builder.addSubPart("BBC1");
          builder.addSubPart("D256");
      builder.endPart();
      Part base = list.getPart("Galaxy Pro 200");
      base.displayInvoice(System.out, 0);
      System.out.println("Resource are: " +
          (base.getResourceList().isValid() ?
              "Valid" : "Invalid"));
      base.getResourceList().displayResources(System.out);
  }
}
```

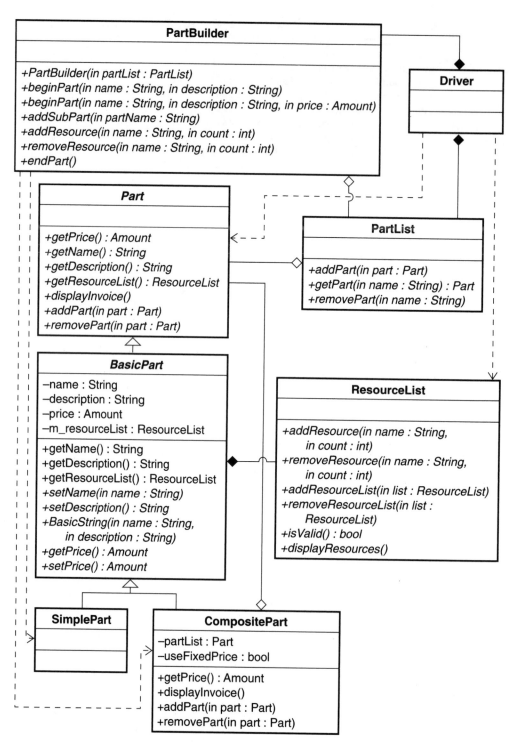

Figure A.1 *The Product Configuration System*

BurgerShop Code

```cpp
// Sandwich.h: interface for the Sandwich class.
//
//////////////////////////////////////////////////////////////////////

#if
    !defined(AFX_SANDWICH_H__675D6587_481A_11D3_BA98_
    00500428B24D__INCLUDED_)
#define
    AFX_SANDWICH_H__675D6587_481A_11D3_BA98_00500428B24D__
    INCLUDED_

#if _MSC_VER > 1000
#pragma once
#endif // _MSC_VER > 1000

typedef double Amount;
#include <string>
using std::string;

class Sandwich
{
public:
    virtual ~Sandwich();
    virtual Amount getPrice() = 0;
    virtual string getName() = 0;
protected:
    Sandwich();
};
```

```
#endif //
      !defined(AFX_SANDWICH_H__675D6587_481A_11D3_BA98_00500428
      B24D__INCLUDED_)
// SandwichDecorator.h: interface for the SandwichDecorator class.
//
//////////////////////////////////////////////////////////////////

#if
      !defined(AFX_SANDWICHDECORATOR_H__675D658A_481A_11D3_BA98_
      00500428B24D__INCLUDED_)
#define
      AFX_SANDWICHDECORATOR_H__675D658A_481A_11D3_BA98_00500428
      B24D__INCLUDED_

#if _MSC_VER > 1000
#pragma once
#endif // _MSC_VER > 1000

#include "Sandwich.h"
#include "NullSandwich.h"

class SandwichDecorator : public Sandwich
{
public:
    virtual ~SandwichDecorator();
protected:
    SandwichDecorator(Sandwich* sandwich);
    inline Sandwich& getSandwich();
    inline virtual string getName();
    inline virtual Amount getPrice();
private:
    SandwichDecorator(const SandwichDecorator& sd); //disable
    Sandwich* m_sandwich;
};

inline Sandwich& SandwichDecorator::getSandwich()
{
    static NullSandwich ns;
    // return either the wrapped sandwich or the null sandwich (if 0)
    return (m_sandwich) ? *m_sandwich : ns ;
}

inline string SandwichDecorator::getName()
{
    return getSandwich().getName();
}

inline Amount SandwichDecorator::getPrice()
{
    return getSandwich().getPrice();
}
```

```cpp
#endif //
      !defined(AFX_SANDWICHDECORATOR_H__675D658A_481A_11D3_BA98_
      00500428B24D__INCLUDED_)
// BasicHamburger.h: interface for the BasicHamburger class.
//
//////////////////////////////////////////////////////////////////////

#if !defined(AFX_BASICHAMBURGER_H__675D658B_481A_11D3_BA98_
      00500428B24D__INCLUDED_)
#define
      AFX_BASICHAMBURGER_H__675D658B_481A_11D3_BA98_00500428B24D__
      INCLUDED_

#if _MSC_VER > 1000
#pragma once
#endif // _MSC_VER > 1000

#include "Sandwich.h"

class BasicHamburger : public Sandwich
{
public:
    BasicHamburger();
    virtual ~BasicHamburger();
    inline virtual Amount getPrice();
    inline virtual string getName();
};

inline string BasicHamburger::getName()
{
    return "Hamburger";
}

inline Amount BasicHamburger::getPrice()
{
    // current price - here for now - future calc
    return 1.79;
}
#endif // !defined(AFX_BASICHAMBURGER_H__675D658B_481A_11D3_BA98_
      00500428B24D__INCLUDED_)

// BasicHamburger.cpp: implementation of the BasicHamburger class.
//
//////////////////////////////////////////////////////////////////////

#include "BasicHamburger.h"
```

```
///////////////////////////////////////////////////////////
// Construction/Destruction
///////////////////////////////////////////////////////////

BasicHamburger::BasicHamburger()
{

}

BasicHamburger::~BasicHamburger()
{

}

// BaconDecorator.h: interface for the BaconDecorator class.
//
///////////////////////////////////////////////////////////

#if
    !defined(AFX_BACONDECORATOR_H__675D6590_481A_11D3_BA98_
    00500428B24D__INCLUDED_)
#define
    AFX_BACONDECORATOR_H__675D6590_481A_11D3_BA98_00500428B24D__
    INCLUDED_

#if _MSC_VER > 1000
#pragma once
#endif // _MSC_VER > 1000

#include "SandwichDecorator.h"


class BaconDecorator : public SandwichDecorator
{
public:
    BaconDecorator(Sandwich* sandwich);
    virtual ~BaconDecorator();
    inline virtual string getName();
    inline virtual Amount getPrice();
};

inline string BaconDecorator::getName()
{
    return getSandwich().getName() + ", bacon";
}

inline Amount BaconDecorator::getPrice()
{
    // current price - here for now - future calc
    return getSandwich().getPrice() + .50;
}
```

```
#endif //
        !defined(AFX_BACONDECORATOR_H__675D6590_481A_11D3_BA98_
        00500428B24D__INCLUDED_)

// BaconDecorator.cpp: implementation of the BaconDecorator class.
//
//////////////////////////////////////////////////////////////////////

#include "stdafx.h"
#include "BaconDecorator.h"

//////////////////////////////////////////////////////////////////////
// Construction/Destruction
//////////////////////////////////////////////////////////////////////

BaconDecorator::BaconDecorator(Sandwich* sandwich):
    SandwichDecorator(sandwich)
{

}

BaconDecorator::~BaconDecorator()
{

}

//
//////////////////////////////////////////////////////////////////////

#if
        !defined(AFX_CHEESEDECORATOR_H__675D6594_481A_11D3_BA98_
        00500428B24D__INCLUDED_)
#define
        AFX_CHEESEDECORATOR_H__675D6594_481A_11D3_BA98_00500428B24D__
        INCLUDED_

#if _MSC_VER > 1000
#pragma once
#endif // _MSC_VER > 1000

#include "SandwichDecorator.h"

class CheeseDecorator : public SandwichDecorator
{
public:
    CheeseDecorator(Sandwich* sandwich);
    virtual ~CheeseDecorator();
    inline virtual string getName();
    inline virtual Amount getPrice();
};
```

```
inline string CheeseDecorator::getName()
{
    return getSandwich().getName() + ", cheese";
}

inline Amount CheeseDecorator::getPrice()
{
    // current price - here for now - future calc
    return getSandwich().getPrice() + .30;
}


#endif //
        !defined(AFX_CHEESEDECORATOR_H__675D6594_481A_11D3_BA98_
        00500428B24D__INCLUDED_)
// CheeseDecorator.cpp: implementation of the CheeseDecorator class.
//
//////////////////////////////////////////////////////////////////

#include "stdafx.h"
#include "CheeseDecorator.h"

//////////////////////////////////////////////////////////////////
// Construction/Destruction
//////////////////////////////////////////////////////////////////

CheeseDecorator::CheeseDecorator(Sandwich* sandwich):
    SandwichDecorator(sandwich)
{

}

CheeseDecorator::~CheeseDecorator()
{

}


// KetchupDecorator.h: interface for the KetchupDecorator class.
//
//////////////////////////////////////////////////////////////////

#if
        !defined(AFX_KETCHUPDECORATOR_H__675D6591_481A_11D3_BA98_
        00500428B24D__INCLUDED_)
#define
        AFX_KETCHUPDECORATOR_H__675D6591_481A_11D3_BA98_00500428B24D__
        INCLUDED_

#if _MSC_VER > 1000
#pragma once
#endif // _MSC_VER > 1000
```

```cpp
#include "SandwichDecorator.h"

class KetchupDecorator : public SandwichDecorator
{
public:
    KetchupDecorator(Sandwich* sandwich);
    virtual ~KetchupDecorator();
    inline virtual string getName();
    inline virtual Amount getPrice();
};

inline string KetchupDecorator::getName()
{
    return getSandwich().getName() + ", ketchup";
}

inline Amount KetchupDecorator::getPrice()
{
    // current price - here for now - future calc
    return getSandwich().getPrice() + 0.0;
}



#endif //
    !defined(AFX_KETCHUPDECORATOR_H__675D6591_481A_11D3_BA98_
    00500428B24D__INCLUDED_)

// KetchupDecorator.cpp: implementation of the KetchupDecorator
    class.
//
//////////////////////////////////////////////////////////////

#include "stdafx.h"
#include "KetchupDecorator.h"

//////////////////////////////////////////////////////////////
// Construction/Destruction
//////////////////////////////////////////////////////////////

KetchupDecorator::KetchupDecorator(Sandwich* sandwich):
    SandwichDecorator(sandwich)
{

}

KetchupDecorator::~KetchupDecorator()
{

}
```

```
// LettuceDecorator.h: interface for the LettuceDecorator class.
//
//////////////////////////////////////////////////////////////

#if
    !defined(AFX_LETTUCEDECORATOR_H__675D658E_481A_11D3_BA98_
    00500428B24D__INCLUDED_)
#define
    AFX_LETTUCEDECORATOR_H__675D658E_481A_11D3_BA98_00500428B24D__
    INCLUDED_

#if _MSC_VER > 1000
#pragma once
#endif // _MSC_VER > 1000

#include "SandwichDecorator.h"

class LettuceDecorator : public SandwichDecorator
{
public:
    LettuceDecorator(Sandwich* sandwich);
    virtual ~LettuceDecorator();
        inline virtual string getName();
        inline virtual Amount getPrice();
};

inline string LettuceDecorator::getName()
{
    return getSandwich().getName() + ", lettuce";
}

inline Amount LettuceDecorator::getPrice()
{
    // current price - here for now - future calc
    return getSandwich().getPrice() + 0.0;
}

#endif //
    !defined(AFX_LETTUCEDECORATOR_H__675D658E_481A_11D3_BA98_
    8_00500428B24D__INCLUDED_)

// LettuceDecorator.cpp: implementation of the
// LettuceDecorator class
//
//////////////////////////////////////////////////////////////

#include "stdafx.h"
#include "LettuceDecorator.h"
```

```
/////////////////////////////////////////////////////////////////
// Construction/Destruction
/////////////////////////////////////////////////////////////////

LettuceDecorator::LettuceDecorator(Sandwich* sandwich):
    SandwichDecorator(sandwich)
{

}

LettuceDecorator::~LettuceDecorator()
{

}

// MayonnaiseDecorator.h: interface for the
// MayonnaiseDecorator class.
//
/////////////////////////////////////////////////////////////////

#if
    !defined(AFX_MAYONNAISEDECORATOR_H__675D658F_481A_11D3_
    BA98_00500428B24D__INCLUDED_)
#define
    AFX_MAYONNAISEDECORATOR_H__675D658F_481A_11D3_BA98_0050
    0428B24D__INCLUDED_

#if _MSC_VER > 1000
#pragma once
#endif // _MSC_VER > 1000

#include "SandwichDecorator.h"

class MayonnaiseDecorator : public SandwichDecorator
{
public:
MayonnaiseDecorator(Sandwich* sandwich);
virtual ~MayonnaiseDecorator();
    inline virtual string getName();
    inline virtual Amount getPrice();
};

inline string MayonnaiseDecorator::getName()
{
    return getSandwich().getName() + ", mayonnaise";
}
```

```
inline Amount MayonnaiseDecorator::getPrice()
{
    // current price - here for now - future calc
    return getSandwich().getPrice() + 0.0;
}


#endif //
      !defined(AFX_MAYONNAISEDECORATOR_H__675D658F_481A_11D3_BA98_
      00500428B24D__INCLUDED_)
// MayonnaiseDecorator.cpp: implementation of the
// MayonnaiseDecorator class.
//
//////////////////////////////////////////////////////////////////////

#include "stdafx.h"
#include "MayonnaiseDecorator.h"

//////////////////////////////////////////////////////////////////////
// Construction/Destruction
//////////////////////////////////////////////////////////////////////

MayonnaiseDecorator::MayonnaiseDecorator(Sandwich* sandwich):
    SandwichDecorator(sandwich)
{

}

MayonnaiseDecorator::~MayonnaiseDecorator()
{

}

// NullSandwich.h: interface for the NullSandwich class.[1]
//
//////////////////////////////////////////////////////////////////////

#if
      !defined(AFX_NULLSANDWICH_H__675D6595_481A_11D3_BA98_00
      500428B24D__INCLUDED_)
```

---

1. So what is this NullSandwich? It doesn't sound too filling, does it? Basically one common observation in programming is that testing the result of an operation for an exception value is time consuming. Basically the Null Pattern (by Bobby Woolf published in *PLoP 3*, March, 1997) encapsulates this exception value as a separate class (or instance) of the type that handles all operations as you would want the exception value to handle. Most commonly, the behavior is to do nothing. This significantly simplifies the client, avoiding the need to test for special-case tests usually at the cost of one extra subclass per interface. This Null Object is normally implemented as a Singleton [Gam, 95] or a Flyweight [Gam, 95] and often is combined with other patterns.

```
#define
      AFX_NULLSANDWICH_H__675D6595_481A_11D3_BA98_00500428
      B24D__INCLUDED_

#if _MSC_VER > 1000
#pragma once
#endif // _MSC_VER > 1000

#include "Sandwich.h"

class NullSandwich : public Sandwich
{
public:
    NullSandwich();
    virtual ~NullSandwich();
    inline virtual Amount getPrice();
    inline virtual string getName();
};

inline Amount NullSandwich::getPrice()
{
    return 0.0;
}

inline string NullSandwich::getName()
{
    return "Nothing";
}

#endif //
      !defined(AFX_NULLSANDWICH_H__675D6595_481A_11D3_BA98_00
      500428B24D__INCLUDED_)
// NullSandwich.cpp: implementation of the NullSandwich class.
//
//////////////////////////////////////////////////////////////////////


#include "stdafx.h"
#include "NullSandwich.h"

//////////////////////////////////////////////////////////////////////
// Construction/Destruction
//////////////////////////////////////////////////////////////////////

NullSandwich::NullSandwich()
{

}

NullSandwich::~NullSandwich()
{
```

```
}

// OnionDecorator.h: interface for the OnionDecorator class.
//
//////////////////////////////////////////////////////////////////////

#if !defined(AFX_ONIONDECORATOR_H__675D658C_481A_11D3_BA98_
       00500428B24D__INCLUDED_)
#define
       AFX_ONIONDECORATOR_H__675D658C_481A_11D3_BA98_00500428
       B24D__INCLUDED_

#if _MSC_VER > 1000
#pragma once
#endif // _MSC_VER > 1000
#include "SandwichDecorator.h"

class OnionDecorator: public SandwichDecorator
{
public:
    OnionDecorator(Sandwich* sandwich);
    virtual ~OnionDecorator();
    inline virtual string getName();
    inline virtual Amount getPrice();
};

inline string OnionDecorator::getName()
{
    return getSandwich().getName() + ", onion";
}

inline Amount OnionDecorator::getPrice()
{
    // current price - here for now - future calc
    return getSandwich().getPrice() + 0.0;
}


#endif //
       !defined(AFX_ONIONDECORATOR_H__675D658C_481A_11D3_BA98_
       00500428B24D__INCLUDED_)
// OnionDecorator.cpp: implementation of the OnionDecorator class.
//
//////////////////////////////////////////////////////////////////////

#include "stdafx.h"
#include "OnionDecorator.h"
```

```
/////////////////////////////////////////////////////////////
// Construction/Destruction
/////////////////////////////////////////////////////////////

OnionDecorator::OnionDecorator(Sandwich* sandwich):
    SandwichDecorator(sandwich)
{

}

OnionDecorator::~OnionDecorator()
{

}

// SalsaDecorator.h: interface for the SalsaDecorator class.
//
/////////////////////////////////////////////////////////////

#if
    !defined(AFX_SALSADECORATOR_H__675D6592_481A_11D3_BA98_
    00500428B24D__INCLUDED_)
#define
    AFX_SALSADECORATOR_H__675D6592_481A_11D3_BA98_00500428B24D__
    INCLUDED_

#if _MSC_VER > 1000
#pragma once
#endif // _MSC_VER > 1000

#include "SandwichDecorator.h"

class SalsaDecorator : public SandwichDecorator
{
public:
    SalsaDecorator(Sandwich* sandwich);
    virtual ~SalsaDecorator();
    inline virtual string getName();
    inline virtual Amount getPrice();
};

inline string SalsaDecorator::getName()
{
    return getSandwich().getName() + ", salsa";
}

inline Amount SalsaDecorator::getPrice()
{
    // current price - here for now - future calc
    return getSandwich().getPrice() + 0.0;
}
```

```
#endif //
      !defined(AFX_SALSADECORATOR_H__675D6592_481A_11D3_BA98_
      00500428B24D__INCLUDED_)
// SalsaDecorator.cpp: implementation of the SalsaDecorator class.
//
//////////////////////////////////////////////////////////////////////

#include "stdafx.h"
#include "SalsaDecorator.h"


//////////////////////////////////////////////////////////////////////
// Construction/Destruction
//////////////////////////////////////////////////////////////////////

SalsaDecorator::SalsaDecorator(Sandwich* sandwich):
    SandwichDecorator(sandwich)
{

}

SalsaDecorator::~SalsaDecorator()
{

}

// TomatoDecorator.h: interface for the TomatoDecorator class.
//
//////////////////////////////////////////////////////////////////////

#if
      !defined(AFX_TOMATODECORATOR_H__675D658D_481A_11D3_BA98_
      00500428B24D__INCLUDED_)
#define
      AFX_TOMATODECORATOR_H__675D658D_481A_11D3_BA98_00500428B24D__
      INCLUDED_

#if _MSC_VER > 1000
#pragma once
#endif // _MSC_VER > 1000

#include "SandwichDecorator.h"

class TomatoDecorator : public SandwichDecorator
{
public:
    TomatoDecorator(Sandwich* sandwich);
    virtual ~TomatoDecorator();
    inline virtual string getName();
    inline virtual Amount getPrice();
};
```

```cpp
inline string TomatoDecorator::getName()
{
    return getSandwich().getName() + ", tomato";
}

inline Amount TomatoDecorator::getPrice()
{
    // current price - here for now - future calc
    return getSandwich().getPrice() + 0.0;
}


#endif //
       !defined(AFX_TOMATODECORATOR_H__675D658D_481A_11D3_BA98_
       00500428B24D__INCLUDED_)

// TomatoDecorator.cpp: implementation of the TomatoDecorator class.
//
//////////////////////////////////////////////////////////////////////

#include "stdafx.h"
#include "TomatoDecorator.h"

//////////////////////////////////////////////////////////////////////
// Construction/Destruction
//////////////////////////////////////////////////////////////////////

TomatoDecorator::TomatoDecorator(Sandwich* sandwich):
    SandwichDecorator(sandwich)
{

}

TomatoDecorator::~TomatoDecorator()
{

}

Main
// BurgerLand.cpp : Defines the entry point for the console
       application.
//
#include <iostream>
#include <memory>

#include "Sandwich.h"
#include "CheeseDecorator.h"
#include "BaconDecorator.h"
#include "TomatoDecorator.h"
#include "BasicHamburger.h"
```

```
int main(int argc, char* argv[])
{
    Sandwich* sand = new CheeseDecorator(new
    BaconDecorator(new TomatoDecorator(new BasicHamburger)));
    std::cout << sand->getName() << " price = $" <<
    sand->getPrice();
    delete sand;
    return 0;
}
```

Following is an example of a simple template definition to avoid coding the many classes:

```
///////////////////////////////////////////////////////////
// TSandwichDecorator.h: interface for the Standard Template
Decorator class.
///////////////////////////////////////////////////////////
#if
    !defined(AFX_TSANDWICHDECORATOR_H__675D6594_481A_11D3_BA98_
    00500428B24D__INCLUDED_)
#define
    AFX_TSANDWICHDECORATOR_H__675D6594_481A_11D3_BA98_00500428
    B24D__INCLUDED_

#if _MSC_VER > 1000
#pragma once
#endif // _MSC_VER > 1000

#include "SandwichDecorator.h"

template <const Amount price>
class TSandwichDecorator : public SandwichDecorator
{
public:
    inline TSandwichDecorator(const string& name, Sandwich*
        sandwich);
    inline virtual ~TSandwichDecorator();
    inline virtual string getName();
    inline virtual Amount getPrice();
private:
    const string m_name;
};


template <const Amount price>
inline TSandwichDecorator<price>::TSandwichDecorator(const
string& name, Sandwich* sandwich):
    SandwichDecorator(sandwich), m_name(name)
{

}
```

```
template <const Amount price>
inline TSandwichDecorator<price>::~TSandwichDecorator()
{

}

template <const Amount price>
inline string TSandwichDecorator<price>::getName()
{
    return getSandwich().getName() + ", " + m_name;
}

template <const Amount price>
inline Amount TSandwichDecorator<price>::getPrice()
{
    // current price - here for now - future calc
    return getSandwich().getPrice() + price;
}


#endif //
        !defined(AFX_TSANDWICHDECORATOR_H__675D6594_481A_11D3_BA98_
        00500428B24D__INCLUDED_)
```

This could then be used as follows:

```
// BurgerLandWithTemplate.cpp : Defines the entry point for the
      console application.
//
#include <iostream>
#include <memory>

#include "Sandwich.h"
#include "CheeseDecorator.h"
#include "BaconDecorator.h"
#include "TomatoDecorator.h"
#include "BasicHamburger.h"
#include "TSandwichDecorator.h"

static const string cheddarName = "Cheddar Cheese";
typedef TSandwichDecorator<.50> CheddarCheeseDecorator;

int main(int argc, char* argv[])
{
    Sandwich* sand = new CheeseDecorator(new
    BaconDecorator(new TomatoDecorator(new
    CheddarCheeseDecorator(cheddarName, new BasicHamburger)))));
    std::cout << sand->getName() << " price = $" <<
    sand->getPrice();
    delete sand;
    return 0;
}
```

BJ.cpp

```cpp
#include <strstream>
#include <list>
#include "deck.h"
#include "card.h"
#include "bjhand.h"
#include "dealhand.h"
#include "simhand.h"
#include "dealer.h"
#include "display.h"
#include "playhand.h"
#include "stddisp.h"

using namespace std;

ostream& operator<<(ostream& s, const Dealer::STATUS& status)
{
   switch (status) {
      case Dealer::BLACKJACK:
         s << "BLACKJACK";
         break;
      case Dealer::WIN:
         s << "WIN";
         break;
      case Dealer::LOSE:
         s << "LOSE";
         break;
```

```
        case Dealer::PUSH:
           s << "PUSH";
           break;
        default:
           throw "Illegal status type";
        }
    return s;
}



void DisplayPlayerResult(const Dealer& dealer, const
      StandardBlackJackHand& bjh)
{
    char buf[255];
    ostrstream output(buf, 255);
    output << dealer.GetPlayerStatus(&bjh) << '\0';
    bjh.GetDisplayer()->DisplayResult(bjh, output.str());
}

void main()
{
    Dealer dealer(1, 30);
    dealer.NewShoe();
    StandardDisplayer disp;
    StandardDealerHand dlr(&disp);
    SimulatedPlayerHand plr1("    Simuplayer", &disp);
    PlayerHand plr2("        Player", &disp);
    dealer.SetDealerHand(&dlr);
    dealer.AssignPlayerHand(&plr1);
    dealer.AssignPlayerHand(&plr2);

    do  {
       dealer.Play();
       // Print results
       dlr.GetDisplayer()->DisplayResult(dlr);
       DisplayPlayerResult(dealer, plr1);
       DisplayPlayerResult(dealer, plr2);
       } while(disp.InquireNewGame());
}
```

bjhand.hpp

```
// Black jack hand header
// Brandon Goldfedder

#ifndef _BLACKJACKHAND
#define _BLACKJACKHAND

#include "card.h"

class BlackJackHand {
public:
    enum TURN_RESULT { BUST, STAND, HIT, DOUBLE_DOWN, SPLIT };
```

```
      inline BlackJackHand();
      virtual inline ~BlackJackHand();
      virtual unsigned int LowCount() const;
        // Count the Ace as lower
      virtual unsigned int HighCount() const;
        // Count the Ace as high
      virtual bool IsBlackJack() const;
        // Is there a blackjack
      virtual unsigned int NumCards() const;
        // How many cards have been dealt
      virtual const Card& GetCard(unsigned int which) const;
        // Get a card user must ensure which <= NumCards
      virtual void AddCard(const Card& card);
        // Deal a card
      virtual void Reset();
        // Clear the hand
      virtual inline bool TookInsurance() const;
      virtual inline bool OfferInsurance();
        // Insurance or even money
      virtual TURN_RESULT TakeTurn();
        // Take a turn
      virtual inline unsigned int NumCardsDealtDown() const;
        // How many cards are dealt down
      virtual bool IsAceShowing() const;
        // Test if an ace is showing as the top card
      virtual inline const char* const GetIdentity() const;
      };


inline BlackJackHand::BlackJackHand()
{
}

inline BlackJackHand::~BlackJackHand()
{
}


inline bool BlackJackHand::TookInsurance() const
{
    return false;
}

inline bool BlackJackHand::OfferInsurance()
{
    return false;
}

inline unsigned int BlackJackHand::NumCardsDealtDown() const
{
    return 0;
}
```

```
inline const char* const BlackJackHand::GetIdentity() const
{
    return "None";
}


#endif
```

card.h

```
// Card header
// Brandon Goldfedder

#ifndef _CARD
#define _CARD

#include <assert.h>

// Represents a standard (one of 52) poker card
// Note that most operations are currently inline to ensure
      the speed
// is the same as if it were an open abstraction
class Card {
public:
    enum SUIT {HEART, DIAMOND, CLUB, SPADE };
    inline Card();
    inline Card(SUIT suit, char value);
    inline Card(const Card& card);
    inline ~Card();
    inline char CardType() const;        // return the current
        card 'A' - 'K'
    inline SUIT Suit() const;            // return the suit
    char SuitAsChar() const;             // return the suit as
        'H','D','S','C'
    inline bool SetSuit(SUIT newSuit);   // Set the suit
        (returns true if successful)
    inline bool SetType(char newType);   // Set the card type
    inline bool IsFaceCard() const;      // is it a face card
        'J','Q','K'
    inline bool IsValueCard() const;     // is it a '2' - 'T'
    inline bool IsAce() const;           // is it an ace
    inline bool IsValid() const;         // test that the card
        type is valid
    inline bool operator < (const Card& rhs) const;  // only
        based on type
    inline bool operator == (const Card& rhs) const; // checks
        both type and suit
    inline Card& operator = (const Card& rhs);
private:
    SUIT suit;
    char value;
    };
```

```
inline Card::Card():
   suit(HEART), value('A')
{
}

inline Card::Card(SUIT suit, char value) :
   suit(suit), value(value)
{
   assert (IsValid());
}

inline Card::Card(const Card& card):
   suit(card.suit), value(card.value)
{
}

inline Card::~Card()
{
}

inline char Card::CardType() const
{
   return value;
}

inline bool Card::SetSuit(SUIT newSuit)
{
   suit = newSuit;
   return true;
}

inline bool Card::SetType(char newType)
{
   value = newType;
   return IsValid();
}

inline Card::SUIT Card::Suit() const
{
   return suit;
}

inline bool Card::IsFaceCard() const
{
   return (value == 'J' || value == 'Q' || value == 'K');
}

inline bool Card::IsValueCard() const
{
   return (value >= '2' || value <= '9' || value == 'T');
}
```

```cpp
inline bool Card::IsAce() const
{
   return value == 'A';
}

inline bool Card::IsValid() const
{
   return IsFaceCard() || IsValueCard() || IsAce();
}


inline bool Card::operator< (const Card& rhs) const
{
   return value < rhs.value;
}

inline bool Card::operator== (const Card& rhs) const
{
   return value == rhs.value && suit == rhs.suit;
}

inline Card& Card::operator= (const Card& rhs)
{
   if (&rhs != this) {
      value = rhs.value;
      suit = rhs.suit;
      }
   return *this;
}

#endif
```

card.cpp

```cpp
// Card Body
// Brandon Goldfedder

#include "card.h"

char Card::SuitAsChar() const
{
   char retval;
   switch (suit) {
      case HEART: retval = 'H'; break;
      case DIAMOND: retval = 'D'; break;
      case SPADE: retval = 'S'; break;
      case CLUB: retval = 'C'; break;
      default: throw "Illegal Card"; // Can not occur
      }
   return retval;
}
```

dealer.h

```cpp
// Dealer header
// Brandon Goldfedder

#include <list>
#include "bjhand.h"
#include "deck.h"

inline void destroy(BlackJackHand**) {} // Needed due to an
      STL issue

class Dealer
{
public:
    enum STATUS {BLACKJACK, WIN, LOSE, PUSH}; // BLACKJACK
    becomes WIN or PUSH if dealer has bj
    Dealer(unsigned int numDecks, unsigned int cutCardPosition);
    ~Dealer();
    void AssignPlayerHand(BlackJackHand* hand);
    void SetDealerHand(BlackJackHand* hand);
    void NewShoe();
    void Play();
    STATUS GetPlayerStatus(const BlackJackHand* hand) const;
        // Hand must be in set to be valid
private:
    const unsigned int numDecks;
    const unsigned int cutCardPosition;
    bool DealCard(BlackJackHand* hand);
    bool ProcessTurn(BlackJackHand* hand); // returns true if
        player still in there
    Deck theDeck;
    std::list<BlackJackHand*> players;
    BlackJackHand* dealer; // dealer will be treated special
};
```

dealer.cpp

```cpp
#include "dealer.h"

bool Dealer::DealCard(BlackJackHand* hand)
{
    Card card;
    if (!theDeck.GetCard(&card))
        throw "Bad Deck";
    hand->AddCard(card);
    return true;
}
```

```cpp
bool Dealer::ProcessTurn(BlackJackHand* hand)
{
   bool doneturn = false;
   bool retval = true;
   BlackJackHand::TURN_RESULT turn;
   while (!doneturn) {
      turn = hand->TakeTurn();
      switch (turn) {
         case BlackJackHand::HIT:
            DealCard(hand);
            break;
         case BlackJackHand::BUST:
            retval = false; // allow fall through
         case BlackJackHand::STAND:
            doneturn = true;
            break;
         case BlackJackHand::DOUBLE_DOWN:
            DealCard(hand);
            retval = hand->HighCount() > 21; // did we bust
            doneturn = true;
            break;
         case BlackJackHand::SPLIT:
            throw "Not implemented";
            // break;
         default:
            throw "Illegal result of move";
      }
   }
   return retval;
}

Dealer::Dealer(unsigned int numDecks, unsigned int cutCardPosition):
   dealer(0), numDecks(numDecks), cutCardPosition(cutCardPosition)
{
}

Dealer::~Dealer()
{
}

void Dealer::AssignPlayerHand(BlackJackHand* hand)
{
   players.push_back(hand);
}

void Dealer::SetDealerHand(BlackJackHand* hand)
{
   dealer = hand;
}
```

```
Dealer::STATUS Dealer::GetPlayerStatus(const BlackJackHand* hand)
   const
{
   Dealer::STATUS status = LOSE;
   unsigned int pCount = hand->HighCount();
   unsigned int dCount = dealer->HighCount();
   // First we handle blackjack as a special case
   if (hand->IsBlackJack()) {
      if (hand->TookInsurance())
         status = WIN;
      else if (dealer->IsBlackJack())
         status = PUSH;
      else
         status = BLACKJACK;
      }
   else if (pCount<= 21) { // We didn't bust
      if (dCount > 21 || pCount > dCount) { // dealer bust or we won
         status = WIN;
         }
      else if (dCount == pCount) // push
         status = PUSH;
      // otherwise the dealer beat us which is the default
      else {
         assert (dCount > pCount);
         }
      }
   return status;
}


void Dealer::NewShoe()
{
   theDeck.BurnIt();
   theDeck.AddDeck();
   theDeck.Shuffle();
}

void Dealer::Play()
{
   if (theDeck.RemainingCards() <= cutCardPosition)
      NewShoe();
   bool somebodyPlaying = false;
   std::list<BlackJackHand*>::iterator currentPlayer;

   // First we clear all the players
   currentPlayer = players.begin();
   while (!(currentPlayer == players.end())) {
      (*currentPlayer)->Reset(); // Reset all the players
      dealer->Reset();
      currentPlayer++;
      }
```

```
   // Now deal 2 cards to each player
   for (int i = 0; i < 2; i++) { // Deal 2 cards to each player
      currentPlayer = players.begin();
      while (!(currentPlayer == players.end())) {
         DealCard(*currentPlayer);
         currentPlayer++;
         }
      DealCard(dealer);
      }

   // First we check for insurance if there is an Ace
   if (dealer->IsAceShowing()) {
      currentPlayer = players.begin();
      while (!(currentPlayer == players.end())) {
         (*currentPlayer)->OfferInsurance(); // We don't care
      about the result
         currentPlayer++;
         }
      }
   if (dealer->IsBlackJack()) {
      }
   else {
      // Process moves
      currentPlayer = players.begin();
      while (!(currentPlayer == players.end())) {
        somebodyPlaying = ProcessTurn(*currentPlayer)
      || somebodyPlaying;
         currentPlayer++;
         }
      if (somebodyPlaying)
         ProcessTurn(dealer);
      }
   }
```

dealhand.h

```
// Dealers hand header
// Brandon Goldfedder

#ifndef _STANDARDDEALERHAND
#define _STANDARDDEALERHAND

#include "stdhand.h"

class StandardDealerHand: public StandardBlackJackHand {
public:
   StandardDealerHand(Displayer *displayer);
   ~StandardDealerHand();
   TURN_RESULT TakeTurn();
```

```
   const char* const GetIdentity() const;
   unsigned int NumCardsDealtDown() const;
   };

#endif
```

dealhand.cpp

```
// Dealers hand body
// Brandon Goldfedder

#include "dealhand.h"
#include "display.h"

StandardDealerHand::StandardDealerHand(Displayer *displayer):
StandardBlackJackHand(displayer)
{
}

StandardDealerHand::~StandardDealerHand()
{
}

BlackJackHand::TURN_RESULT StandardDealerHand::TakeTurn()
{
   TURN_RESULT result = STAND;
   if (HighCount() < 17)
      result = HIT;
   else if (HighCount() > 21)
      result = BUST;
   GetDisplayer()->DisplayTurn(*this, result);
   return result;
}

const char* const StandardDealerHand::GetIdentity() const
{
   return "Dealer"; // should ensure static allocation
}


unsigned int StandardDealerHand::NumCardsDealtDown() const
{
   return 1;
}
```

deck.h

```
// Deck header
// Brandon Goldfedder

#ifndef _DECK
#define _DECK
```

```cpp
#include <vector>
#include "card.h"

// Deck represents a group of >=0 sets of 52 cards

class Deck {
public:
    Deck();
    ~Deck();
    void BurnIt(); // Destroy all cards in the decks
    void AddDeck(unsigned int numDecks = 1); // Adds numDecks
        of Cards into the Deck, does not shuffle it in
    void Shuffle(); // Shuffle all cards currently in the deck
    bool GetCard(Card* card); // Draw the top card (if any) from
        the deck, return if this was successful (any cards left)
    unsigned int RemainingCards();
private:
    std::vector<Card> actualDeck; // We will use a deque to
    // store the set of cards
    };

#endif
```

deck.cpp

```cpp
// Deck body
// Brandon Goldfedder

#include <algorithm>
#include "deck.h"
Deck::Deck()
{
}

Deck::~Deck()
{
}

void Deck::BurnIt()
{
    actualDeck.erase(actualDeck.begin(), actualDeck.end());
}

void Deck::AddDeck(unsigned int numDecks)
{
    const unsigned int NUMVALUES = 13;
    const unsigned int NUMSUITS = 4;
    const char cardValues[NUMVALUES] = {'A', '2', '3', '4',
        '5', '6', '7', '8', '9', 'T', 'J', 'Q', 'K'};
    const Card::SUIT suitValues[NUMSUITS] = { Card::HEART,
        Card::DIAMOND, Card::SPADE, Card::CLUB};
```

```
        Card crd;
        for (int count = 0; count < numDecks; count++) {
            for (int i = 0; i < NUMSUITS; i++) {
                crd.SetSuit(suitValues[i]);
                for (int j = 0; j < NUMVALUES; j++) {
                    crd.SetType(cardValues[j]);
                    actualDeck.push_back(crd);
                }
            }
        }
    }

    void Deck::Shuffle()
    {
        std::random_shuffle(actualDeck.begin(), actualDeck.end());
    }

    bool Deck::GetCard(Card* card)
    {
        bool retval = !actualDeck.empty();
        if (retval) {
            *card = actualDeck.back();
            actualDeck.pop_back();
        }
        return retval;
    }

    unsigned int Deck::RemainingCards()
    {
        return actualDeck.size();
    }
```

display.h

```
    // Display Header
    // Brandon Goldfedder

    #ifndef _DISPLAYER
    #define _DISPLAYER

    #include "bjhand.h"

    // The Displayer class forms the interface for all I/O in the system
    // Note the use of default null functions to provide NOP behavior
        class Displayer {
    public:
        Displayer() {}
        virtual ~Displayer() {}
        virtual void Reset(const BlackJackHand& hand) {}
        virtual void DrawCard(const BlackJackHand& hand, const
            Card& card) {}
```

```
        virtual void DisplayTurn(const BlackJackHand& hand,
            BlackJackHand::TURN_RESULT turn) {}
        virtual void DisplayResult(const BlackJackHand& hand, const
            char* result = 0) {} // Display the result - use a 0 for
            result to just display total
        virtual bool InquireInsurance(const BlackJackHand& hand) {
            return false;}
        virtual BlackJackHand::TURN_RESULT InquireTurn(const
            BlackJackHand& hand, bool mayDouble = false, bool maySplit =
            false) = 0;
        virtual bool InquireNewGame() { return false; } // Ask for
            a new game
        };

    #endif
```

playhand.h

```
    // Players hand header
    // Brandon Goldfedder

    #ifndef _PLAYERHAND
    #define _PLAYERHAND

    #include "stdhand.h"

    class PlayerHand: public StandardBlackJackHand {
    public:
        PlayerHand(const char* name, Displayer *displayer);
        ~PlayerHand();
        TURN_RESULT TakeTurn();
        bool TookInsurance() const;
        bool OfferInsurance();
        const char* const GetIdentity() const;
    private:
        bool tookInsurance;
        char* id;
        };

    #endif
```

playhand.cpp

```
    // Players hand body
    // Brandon Goldfedder

    #include "playhand.h"
    #include "display.h"
    #include <string.h>
    PlayerHand::PlayerHand(const char* name, Displayer
        *displayer): StandardBlackJackHand(displayer)
```

```cpp
{
    id = new char[strlen(name) + 1];
    strcpy(id, name);
}

PlayerHand::~PlayerHand()
{
    delete[] id;
}

BlackJackHand::TURN_RESULT PlayerHand::TakeTurn()
{
    TURN_RESULT result = BUST;
    bool mayDouble = false;
    bool maySplit = false;
    if (NumCards() == 2) {
        unsigned int count = HighCount();
        mayDouble = (count == 9 || count == 10 || count == 11);
        maySplit = IsSplitable();
        }
    if (HighCount() <= 21)
        result = GetDisplayer()->InquireTurn(*this, mayDouble,
        maySplit);
    GetDisplayer()->DisplayTurn(*this, result);
    return result;
}

bool PlayerHand::TookInsurance() const
{
    return tookInsurance;
}

bool PlayerHand::OfferInsurance()
{
    tookInsurance = GetDisplayer()->InquireInsurance(*this);
    return tookInsurance;
}

const char* const PlayerHand::GetIdentity() const
{
    return id;
}
```

Random.h

```
/*
 *
 * Copyright (c) 1994
 * Hewlett-Packard Company
 *
```

```
    * Permission to use, copy, modify, distribute, and sell this
          software
    * and its documentation for any purpose is hereby granted
          without fee,
    * provided that the above copyright notice appear in all copies and
    * that both that copyright notice and this permission notice appear
    * in supporting documentation.  Hewlett-Packard Company makes no
    * representations about the suitability of this software for any
    * purpose.  It is provided "as is" without express or implied
          warranty.
    *
    */

#include <stddef.h>

// #define __SEED 161803398
// Modified by Brandon
#include <time.h>
time_t t;
#define __SEED (unsigned long) (unsigned) time(&t)

class __random_generator {
protected:
    unsigned long table[55];
    size_t index1;
    size_t index2;
public:
    unsigned long operator()(unsigned long limit) {
        index1 = (index1 + 1) % 55;
        index2 = (index2 + 1) % 55;
        table[index1] = table[index1] - table[index2];
        return table[index1] % limit;
    }
    void seed(unsigned long j);
    __random_generator(unsigned long j) { seed(j); }
};

void __random_generator::seed(unsigned long j) {
    unsigned long k = 1;
    table[54] = j;
    for (size_t i = 0; i < 54; i++) {
        size_t ii = 21 * i % 55;
        table[ii] = k;
        k = j - k;
        j = table[ii];
    }
    for (int loop = 0; loop < 4; loop++) {
        for (int i = 0; i < 55; i++)
            table[i] = table[i] - table[(1 + i + 30) % 55];
```

```
        }
        index1 = 0;
        index2 = 31;
    }

    __random_generator rd(__SEED);

    unsigned long __long_random(unsigned long limit) {
        return rd(limit);
    }
```

simhand.h

```
// Simulated Player  hand header
// Brandon Goldfedder

#ifndef _SIMULATEDPLAYERHAND
#define _SIMULATEDPLAYERHAND

#include "stdhand.h"

class SimulatedPlayerHand: public StandardBlackJackHand {
public:
    SimulatedPlayerHand(const char* name, Displayer
    *displayer);
    ~SimulatedPlayerHand();
    TURN_RESULT TakeTurn();
    const char* const GetIdentity() const;
private:
    char* id;
    };

#endif
```

simhand.cpp

```
// Simulated Player hand body
// Brandon Goldfedder

#include <string.h>
#include "simhand.h"
#include "display.h"

SimulatedPlayerHand::SimulatedPlayerHand(const char* name,
        Displayer *displayer): StandardBlackJackHand(displayer)
{
    id = new char[strlen(name) + 1];
    strcpy(id, name);
}
```

```
SimulatedPlayerHand::~SimulatedPlayerHand()
{
   delete[] id;
}

const char* const SimulatedPlayerHand::GetIdentity() const
{
   return id;
}

BlackJackHand::TURN_RESULT SimulatedPlayerHand::TakeTurn()
{
   TURN_RESULT result = STAND;
   if (HighCount() < 17)
      result = HIT;
   else if (HighCount() > 21)
      result = BUST;
   GetDisplayer()->DisplayTurn(*this, result);
   return result;
}
```

stddisp.h

```
#ifndef _STANDARDDISPLAYER
#define _STANDARDDISPLAYER

#include "bjhand.h"
#include "display.h"

class StandardDisplayer: public Displayer {
public:
   StandardDisplayer();
   ~StandardDisplayer();
   void DrawCard(const BlackJackHand& hand, const Card& card);
   void DisplayTurn(const BlackJackHand& hand,
      BlackJackHand::TURN_RESULT turn);
   void DisplayResult(const BlackJackHand& hand, const char*
      result = 0);
   bool InquireInsurance(const BlackJackHand& hand);
   BlackJackHand::TURN_RESULT InquireTurn(const BlackJackHand& hand,
      bool mayDouble = false, bool maySplit = false);
   bool InquireNewGame();
private:
   void DisplayCards(const BlackJackHand& hand);
   };

#endif
```

stddisp.cpp

```cpp
#include <iostream.h>
#include "stddisp.h"
#include "dealer.h"
#include <ctype.h> // for tolower

ostream& operator<<(ostream& s, const Card& card)
{
    s << card.CardType() << card.SuitAsChar();
    return s;
}

istream& operator>>(istream& s, BlackJackHand::TURN_RESULT& result)
{
    char c = '\0';
    while (c != 'h' && c != 's' && c != 'd')
        s >> c;
    switch (c) {
        case 'h':
            result = BlackJackHand::HIT;
            break;
        case 'd':
            result = BlackJackHand::DOUBLE_DOWN;
            break;
        case 's':
            result = BlackJackHand::STAND;
            break;
        case 'p':
            result = BlackJackHand::SPLIT;
            break;
        default:
            throw "Undefined!";
        }
    return s;
}

ostream& operator<<(ostream& s, const BlackJackHand::TURN_RESULT&
    result)
{
    switch (result) {
        case BlackJackHand::HIT:
            s << "HIT";
            break;
        case BlackJackHand::BUST:
            s << "BUST";
            break;
        case BlackJackHand::STAND:
            s << "STAND";
            break;
```

```
            case BlackJackHand::DOUBLE_DOWN:
               s << "DOUBLE_DOWN";
               break;
            case BlackJackHand::SPLIT:
               s << "SPLIT";
               break;
            default:
               throw "Illegal result of move";
            }
     return s;
}

void StandardDisplayer::DisplayCards(const BlackJackHand& hand)
{
   int numCards = hand.NumCards();
   for (int i = 0; i < numCards; i++)
      cout << hand.GetCard(i) << " ";
}


StandardDisplayer::StandardDisplayer()
{
}

StandardDisplayer::~StandardDisplayer()
{
}

void StandardDisplayer::DrawCard(const BlackJackHand& hand,
        const Card& card)
{
   cout << hand.GetIdentity() << " : dealt a ";
   if (hand.NumCards() < hand.NumCardsDealtDown())
      cout <<  "XX";
   else
      cout <<  card;
   cout << '\n';
}

void StandardDisplayer::DisplayTurn(const BlackJackHand& hand,
        BlackJackHand::TURN_RESULT turn)
{
   cout << hand.GetIdentity() << "(" << hand.LowCount() << "/"
        << hand.HighCount() << "): " << turn << ":" ;
   DisplayCards(hand);
   cout << '\n';
}

void StandardDisplayer::DisplayResult(const BlackJackHand&
        hand, const char* result)
```

```cpp
{
    cout << hand.GetIdentity() << " ( " <<  hand.HighCount() << ")";
    if (result)
        cout << ": resulted with a  " << result << '\n';
    else
        cout << '\n';
}

bool StandardDisplayer::InquireInsurance(const BlackJackHand& hand)
{
    char insurance = '\0';
    while (insurance != 'y' && insurance != 'n') {
        cout << hand.GetIdentity() << ": Insurance (y/n)? \n";
        cin >> insurance;
        }
    return insurance == 'y';
}

BlackJackHand::TURN_RESULT StandardDisplayer::InquireTurn
            (const BlackJackHand& hand, bool mayDouble, bool
             maySplit)
{
    BlackJackHand::TURN_RESULT result;
    cout << hand.GetIdentity() << "(" << hand.LowCount() << "/"
        << hand.HighCount() << ") :";
    DisplayCards(hand);
    cout << '\n';
    cout << "What do you want to do H-Hit, S-Stand ";
    if (mayDouble)
        cout << "D-DoubleDown ";
    if (maySplit)
        cout << "P-Split";
    cout << '\n';
    cin >> result;
    return result;
}

bool StandardDisplayer::InquireNewGame()
{
    char c = ' ';
    while (c != 'y' && c != 'n'){
        cout << "New Game? ";
        cin >> c;
        c = tolower(c);
        }
    return c == 'y';
}
```

stdhand.h

```cpp
// StandardBlack jack hand header
// Brandon Goldfedder

#ifndef _STANDARDBLACKJACKHAND
#define _STANDARDBLACKJACKHAND

#include "bjhand.h"
#include <deque>

class Displayer; // Forward reference to avoid circular
                 // references'

class StandardBlackJackHand: public BlackJackHand {
public:
   StandardBlackJackHand(Displayer* displayer);
   virtual ~StandardBlackJackHand();
   unsigned int LowCount() const;    // Count the Ace as lower
   unsigned int HighCount() const;   // Count the Ace as high
   bool IsBlackJack() const;         // Is there a blackjack
   bool IsSplitable() const;         // Is there a blackjack
   unsigned int NumCards() const;    // How many cards have been
       dealt
   const Card& GetCard(unsigned int which) const; // Get a
       card user must ensure which <= NumCards
   void AddCard(const Card& card);   // Deal a card
   void Reset();                              // Clear the hand
   bool IsAceShowing() const;                 // Test if an ace is
showing as the top card
   inline Displayer* GetDisplayer() const;    // Allow access
       to the underlying displayer
private:
   unsigned int TotalCardCount(bool highCount) const;
       // Count one card
   unsigned int SingleCardCount(const Card& card, bool highCount)
       const;    // Count all the cards in the hand
   Displayer* displayer;
   std::deque<Card> hand;
   };

inline Displayer* StandardBlackJackHand::GetDisplayer() const
{
   return displayer;
}

#endif
```

stdhand.cpp

```
// Standard Black jack hand body
// Brandon Goldfedder

#include <assert.h>
#include "stdhand.h"
#include "display.h"

unsigned int StandardBlackJackHand::SingleCardCount(const
      Card& card, bool highCount) const
{
   unsigned int count = 0;
   if (card.IsAce())
      count += (highCount ? 11 : 1);
   else if (card.IsFaceCard() || card.CardType() == 'T')
      count += 10;
   else {
      assert (card.IsValueCard());
      count = count + card.CardType() - '0';
      }
   return count;
}


unsigned int StandardBlackJackHand::TotalCardCount(bool highCount)
    const
{
   unsigned int count = 0;
   unsigned int numAces = 0;
   std::deque<Card>::const_iterator card = hand.begin();
   while (!(card == hand.end())) {
      if ((*card).IsAce()) // Count the aces
         numAces++;
      count += SingleCardCount(*card, false); // compute low
      WAS highCount && count < 11;
      card++;
      }
   // Count one ace at the end if we are highcounting
   if (highCount && count <= 11 && numAces > 0)
      count += 10;
   return count;
}


StandardBlackJackHand::StandardBlackJackHand(Displayer* displayer):
     displayer(displayer)
{
}
```

```
StandardBlackJackHand::~StandardBlackJackHand()
{
}

void StandardBlackJackHand::AddCard(const Card& card)
{
   displayer->DrawCard(*this, card);
   hand.push_back(card);
}

void StandardBlackJackHand::Reset()
{
   displayer->Reset(*this);
   hand.erase(hand.begin(), hand.end());
}

bool StandardBlackJackHand::IsAceShowing() const
{
   return hand.back().IsAce();
}

bool StandardBlackJackHand::IsBlackJack() const
{
   return ((hand.size() == 2) && (HighCount() == 21));
}

bool StandardBlackJackHand::IsSplitable() const
{
   return ((hand.size() == 2) && (hand.front().CardType() ==
      hand.back().CardType()));
}

unsigned int StandardBlackJackHand::NumCards() const
{
   return hand.size();
}

const Card& StandardBlackJackHand::GetCard(unsigned int which) const
{
   assert (which <= hand.size());
   return hand.begin()[which];
}

unsigned int StandardBlackJackHand::LowCount() const
{
   return TotalCardCount(false);
}

unsigned int StandardBlackJackHand::HighCount() const
{
   return TotalCardCount(true);
}
```

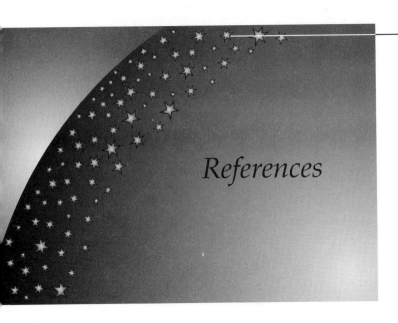

References

[Ale, 64] C. Alexander. *Notes on the Synthesis of Form.* Harvard University Press, Cambridge, MA: 1964.

[Ale, 77] C. Alexander. *A Pattern Language: Towns, Buildings, Constructions.* Harvard University Press, Cambridge, MA: 1977.

[Ale, 79] C. Alexander. *The Timeless Way of Building.* Harvard University Press, Cambridge, MA: 1979.

[Alf, 95] C. Alfred and S.J. Mellor. "Observations on the Role of Patterns in Object-Oriented Software Development." *OBJECT Magazine,* May 1995.

[Bec, 00] K. Beck. *Extreme Programming Explained: Embrace Change,* Addison-Wesley, Boston, MA: 2000.

[Boo, 96] G. Booch. *Object Solutions: Managing the Object-Oriented Project.* Addison-Wesley, Reading, MA: 1996.

[Boo, 99] G. Booch, J. Rumbaugh, I. Jacobson. *The Unified Modeling Language User Guide.* Addison-Wesley, Reading, MA: 1999.

[Bus, 96] F. Buschmann, et al. *Pattern-Oriented Software Architecure: A System of Patterns.* John Wiley & Sons, West Sussex, England: 1996.

[Cop, 92] J. Coplien. *Advanced C++ Programming Styles and Idioms.* Addison-Wesley, Reading, MA: 1992.

[Cop, 94] J. Coplien. "Software Design Patterns: Common Questions and Answers." Posted paper, 1994.

[Cop, 95] J. Coplien and D. Schmidt. *Pattern Languages of Program Design.* Addison-Wesley, Reading, MA: 1995.

[Cop, 98] J. Coplien. *Multi-Paradigm Design for C++.* Addison-Wesley, Reading, MA: 1999.

[Fit, 94]   Visio Chess Template: Dennis K. Fitzgerald CIS: 72627,1442 2/94.

[Fow, 97a]   M. Fowler. *Analysis Patterns: Reusable Object Models.* Addison-Wesley, Reading, MA: 1997.

[Fow, 97]   M. Fowler, K. Scott. *UML Distilled: Applying the Standard Object Modeling Language.* Addison-Wesley, Reading, MA: 1997.

[Fow, 99]   M. Fowler, et al. *Refactoring: Improving the Design of Existing Code.* Addison-Wesley, Reading, MA: 1999.

[Gab, 96]   R. Gabriel. *Patterns of Software.* Oxford University Press, New York: 1996.

[Gam, 95]   E. Gamma, R. Helm, R. Johnson, J. Vlissides, *Design Patterns: Elements of Reusable Object-Oriented Software.* Addison-Wesley, Reading, MA: 1995.

[Gam, 96]   E. Gamma. "Applying Design Patterns in Java," *Java Report,* Volume 1, No. 6. November/December 1996.

[Gol, 96]   B. Goldfedder, L. Rising, "A Training Experience with Patterns." *Communications of the ACM,* 39:10, October 1996.

[Gol, 98]   "Patterns and System Development", *Advances in Computers,* Volume 47: 1998. ISBN 0-12-012147-6.

[Gra, 98]   M. Grand. *Patterns in Java.* Volume 1, John Wiley & Sons, New York: 1998.

[Jac, 99]   I. Jacobson, G. Booch, J. Rumbaugh. *The Unified Software Development Process.* Addison-Wesley, Reading, MA: 1999.

[Lis, 88]   B. Liskov. "Data Abstraction and Hierachy." SIGPLAN Notices 23,5; May 1988.

[Mar, 98]   R. Martin, D. Riehl, and F. Bushchmann. *Pattern Language of Program Design 3.* Addison-Wesley, Reading, MA: 1998.

[McC, 95]   J. McCarthy. *Dynamics of Software Development.* Microsoft Press: 1995.

[Mey, 88]   B. Meyers. *Object-Oriented Software Construction.* Prentice-Hall, Englewood Cliffs, NJ: 1988.

[Mey, 96]   S. Meyers, *More Effective C++: 35 New Ways to Improve Your Programs and Designs.* Addison-Wesley, Reading, MA: 1996.

[Opd, 92]   William F. Opdyke. *Refactoring Object-Oriented Frameworks.* Ph.D. thesis, University of Illinois at Urbana-Champaign, 1992.

[Ris, 00]   L. Rising. *The Pattern Almanac.* Addison-Wesley, Reading, MA: 2000.

[Rum, 99]   J. Rumbaugh, I. Jacobson, G. Booch. *The Unified Modeling Language Reference Manual.* Addison-Wesley, Reading, MA: 1999.

[Sch, 00]   D. Shmidt, et al. *Pattern-Oriented Software Architecure.* Volume 2: Patterns for Concurrent and Networked Objects. John Wiley & Sons, West Sussex, England: 2000.

[Tal, 94]   "Taligent White Paper on Building Object-Oriented Frameworks." Taligent, Inc.: 1994.

[Vil, 95a]   Panu Viljamaa. "The Patterns Business: Impressions from PLoP–94." ACM Software Engineering Notes, Volume 20, No. 1: Jan. 1995.

Vli, 95b]   J. Vlissides. "Reverse Architure." Position Paper Dagstuhl Seminar 9508: 1995.

[Vli, 96a]   J. Vlissides. "To Kill a Singleton." *C++ Report*. June 1996.

[Vli, 96b]   J. Vlissides, J. Coplien, and N. Kerth. *Pattern Language of Program Design 2*. Addison-Wesley, Reading, MA: 1996.

[Vli, 98]   J. Vlissides. *Pattern Hatching: Design Patterns Applied*. Addision-Wesley, Reading, MA: 1998.

[Zim, 95]   W. Zimmer, contributor. "Relationships Between Design Patterns," *Pattern Language of Program Design*. Addison-Wesley, Reading, MA: 1995.

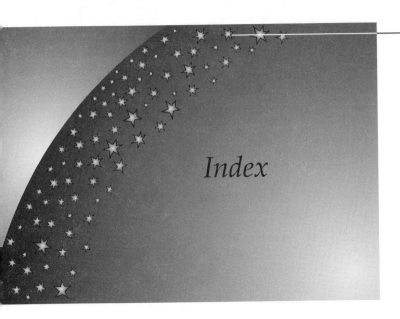

Index

A

Abstract Data Types (ADT), 31–34
Abstract Factory, 99
Abstraction
   Abstract Class, 36, 38
   Abstract Strategy patterns, 103
   variations and, 94
Account example, 78–84
ACM, 28
Ada 83, 17
Adapter, 99
ADT (Abstract Data Types), 31–34
Advanced C++: Programming Style and
   Idioms, 28
Alexander, Christopher, 2, 28
Aliases, 4, 9
Analysis Patterns: Reusable Object Models, 28
Architecture
   building blocks of, 7–8
   flexibility, 92
   Pattern-Oriented software, 28–29
   present *v.* future needs, 3–4
   system variance and, 91–92

B

Background, 1–2
Base Class, 50
BEA Jolt, 42
Beck, Kent, 5, 13, 28
Berczuk, Steve, 2*n*
Binary search, 23
Blackjack example
   architecture flexibility, 92
   codes overall, 143–166
   creating hinge points, 87–91
   language choices, 92–94
   restarting at lower levels, 94–95
   understanding requirements, 86–87
   using supporting patterns, 91–92
Booch, Grady, 28, 43
Bridge, 14, 15, 22, 99
Build for Today, Design for Tomorrow, 2*n*, 4
Builder, 54–59, 99, 120–121
BurgerShop example
   codes, 125–141
   getPrice, 66–71
   modeling, 61–71

BurgerShop example (*continued*)
    overview, 61
    reflections, 72–73
    simplifications, 73–75
    summary, 75
    templates, 140–141
Buschmann, Frank, 28

C

C+, 36
C++
    building flexibility, 3
    BurgerShop example, 71
    checking, 92
    interfaces, 36
    object-orientation, 17
    passing parameters, 18–19
    pattern compatibility, 77–78
    Standard Library, 18
C languages, 77, 78
Chain of Responsibility, 55, 99
Change management, 23–27
Class
    Abstract, 36, 38
    base, 50
    Class explosion, 61–75
    CompositePart, 50
    Concrete, 36, 38, 50, 91
    implementing interfaces, 33–34, 35
    middle, 89
Coad, Peter, 28
COBOL, 17, 36, 78
Codes
    Blackjack. *see* Blackjack example
    BurgerShop. *see* BurgerShop example
    Product. *see* Product codes
Colors, 24, 26–27
Command, 99
Commonality, 88
Communication skills, 20–22
Components, 41–42
Composite
    patterns, 48–55, 75
    varies, 99
Concrete Class, 36, 38, 92
Concrete Strategy patterns, 103

Configuration. *See also* Product Configuration example
    defined, 48
    resources, 51–54
Context
    building or extending systems, 2
    defined, 12–13
    feature use and removal, 14
    phasing out features, 16
    Recyle Bin, 14
    resource allocation, 14
    selecting state, 26
Coplien, Jim, 28, 88
CORBA, 41–42
Creational patterns, 91–92, 100
Cunningham, Ward, 28

D

Data elements, 38
Decorator
    BurgerShop example, 66–75
    Class explosion, 63–66
    logging mechanisms, 95
    tracing logging capability example, 50
    varies, 99
Delegation, 39, 41
Design Patterns: Elements of Reusable Object-Oriented Software, 28
Design Rationale, 13, 14, 17
Development. *See* System development
Displayers, 91, 94, 96
Documentation, 22–23, 98
Domain-specific concepts, 17
Drivers, 56, 118–119, 121–124

E

ECOOP 93, 28
EJB (Enterprise Java Beans), 41
Elegance, 97
Encapsulation, 31, 38–39
Enterprise Java Beans (EJB), 41
Enumerator, 59
ErrorHandlers, 103–104
Evolution of systems. *See* Maintenance

Extensible software development, 23–27
Extreme Programming, 4–5
Extreme Programming Explained:
    Embrace (XP), 4

F

Facade, 99
Factory Method, 92, 99
Flyweight patterns, 25, 99, 104, 134*n*
Force Resolution, 13
Forces
    defined, 10–12
    High Road Development example, 2–3
    importance of features to users, 16
    Recyle Bin, 14
Form, 9–13
FORTRAN, 17–18
Fowler, Martin, 28, 43, 100
Future *v.* present needs, 2–5

G

Gamma, Erich, 28
Generalization, 34
GOF patterns, 98, 99
Goldfedder, Brandon
    e-mail address, 110
    Recycle Bin pattern, 15
    Scream Test pattern, 17

H

Helm, Richard, 28
Help desks, 17
Hewlett-Packard Company, 157–158
High Road Development, 2–5, 87
Hillside Group, 28
Hinge points, 87–91, 98–100
History
    author's background, 1–2
    of patterns, 28
    of programming languages, 17–18
Hotspot, 15

I

Implementation
    interfaces, 33–35, 36
    languages, 18–19
    present *v.* future needs, 3–4
    system development, 92–94
Inheritance, 34–41, 61–63, 94
Interfaces, 33–34, 35, 36
Interpreter, 99
Iterator, 59, 99

J

Java
    Account example, 82–84
    common libraries, 18
    components, 42
    CompositePart.java, 114–115
    Hotspot Java, 15
    interfaces, 36
    Java Application Servers, 42
    Observer, 82–84
    pattern compatibility, 77
    Product Configuration System, 59
Johnson, Ralph, 28
Jolt, 42
Just In Time, 4

K

Kernel requests, 14
Knowledge transfer, 27

L

Leaf nodes, 49
LEGO sets, 7
Libraries
    reuse, 17–18, 23
    shared, 41
    thread, 77
Liskov, B., 36

M

Maintenance
  adding new patterns, 100
  adding or changing behaviors, 99–100
  ErrorHandlers, 103–104
  evolution, 97
  example, 101
  MsgBoxes, 104
  overview, 97–98
  refactoring, 100, 106–108
  SNMP alerts, 104
  standard design and coding, 100
  Strategy patterns, 101–106
  summary, 106–108
  testing and deployment, 100–101
  understanding change and its impact,
    98–99
Mediator, 99
Memento, 99
Memory, 14–15
Meyers, Scott, 24, 38
Microsoft, 41, 78
Middle Class, 89
Modules, 31
MsgBoxes, 104
Multi-Paradigm Design for C++, 88

N

Names, 9
Notes on the Synthesis of Form, 28
Null Object, 134*n*
Null pattern, 134*n*

O

Object-Based Design, 32
Object-orientation. *See* OO
Object-Oriented Design (OOD), 31
Observer, 8–9, 79–84, 99
OMG, 41
OO, 31–42
  change management, 23
  components, 41–42
  inheritance, 34–40

  introduction, 31–34
    summary, 42–43
OOD techniques, 31
Opdyke, William, 100
Open-Closed Principle, 24, 46, 98

P

Palm Pilot, 1
Parameterization, 36
Parnas, David, 31
PartList, 102
Parts
  building, 54–59
  defined, 47, 50
  hierarchy, 51, 54
Pattern Language, A, 28
Pattern Language of Programming (PLoP)
    Conference, 28
Pattern-Oriented Software Architecture: A
    System of Patterns, 28
Patterns
  Account example, 78–84
  architecture, 7–8
  Builder, 54–59
  Composite, 48–55
  Creational, 91–92, 100
  Decorator, 50, 95
  defined, 7
  documentation, 22–23
  extensible software development, 23–27
  Factory Method, 92
  Flyweight, 25, 104, 134*n*
  form, 9–13
  GOF, 98, 99
  High Road Development, 2–5
  history of, 28
  independence from programming lan-
    guages, 77–84
  Null, 134*n*
  Observer, 8–9, 79–84
  present *v.* future needs, 2–5
  programming languages, 17–22, 77–84
  proxy, 9
  Recycle Bin, 13–16
  refactoring, 100
  Scream Test, 16–17

State, 25–27, 50, 101, 104
Strategy, 75, 89, 101–106
summary, 109–110
system development, 85–95
system maintenance, 97–108
PL-SQL, 78
PLoP 3, 134*n*
PLoP (Pattern Language of Programming)
Conference, 28
Present *v.* future needs, 2–5
Pricing, 66–71, 75, 101, 104–106
Problem
creating sales support system, 45–47
defined, 9–10
determining if system aspects are in use, 16
existing *v.* future requirements, 17–18
Product Configuration example
builder pattern, 55–59
composite, 49–55
introduction, 45
observations, 48
problem definition, 45–47
solution, 47–48
system maintenance, 101
Programming languages. *See also* by individual languages
interfaces, 36
OO. *see* OO
pattern independence and compatibility, 77–84
patterns as language of design, 17–22
UML (Unified Modeling Language), 31–34, 43
Prototype, 99
Proxy, 9, 99
Publisher Subscriber, 8–9
Push *v.* Pull models, 9

R

RAD, 4
Radio Shack, 1
Recycle Bin, 13–16
Refactoring, 4–5, 100, 106–108
Refactoring: Improving the Design of Existing Code, 28
Reification, 24

Requirements, 86–87
Resources
configuration, 51–54
creation and destruction of, 13–16
defined, 48
Resulting Context
defined, 13
existing *v.* future requirements, 3
Recycle Bin, 14
understanding importance of features, 16
Reuse library, 17–18, 23
Review process, 35
Rising, Linda, 28

S

Scream Test, 16–17
Silver Bullets, 28
SimplePart, 50, 58–59, 102, 105
SimplePart.java, 113
Singleton, 25, 99, 134*n*
SmallTalk, 17, 28, 100
SNMP alerts, 104
Solutions
creating sales support system, 47–48
defined, 13
design *v.* implementation, 3
Recycle Bin, 14
temporary disabling of features, 16
State patterns
behavior and internal state change, 24, 25–27
pricing calculations, 101, 104
Product Configuration, 50
varies, 99
Strategy patterns, 89, 101–106
Abstract, 103
Concrete, 103
decorator use, 75
varies, 99
Structure, 13
Substitution Principle, 36
Switch scheduling systems, 21
System development
building from scratch, 85–86
coding, 92–94
hinge points for change, 87–91

System development (*continued*)
   implementation, 92–94
   restarting at lower levels, 94–95
   sanity checks, 92
   summary, 95
   supporting patterns, 91–92
   understanding requirements, 86–87
System Maintenance. *See* Maintenance

T

Taligent, Inc., 23
Team-based approaches, 21–22
Template Method, 99, 140–141
Templates, 140–141
The Pattern Almanac, 28
Thread libraries, 77
Total Commissions Systems (TCS), 4
Training, 27
Transact-SQL, 78
Transaction Monitors, 41–42
Type (interface), 33–35

U

UML Distilled, 43

UML (Unified Modeling Language), 31,
   33–34, 43
UML Users Guide, 43
UNIX systems, 14, 21
Unknowns, 12, 86–87

V

Variance, 88–91, 99
Varies
   defined, 13
   GOF patterns, 99
   object structure and composition, 49
   Observer patterns, 8
   State pattern, 25
Visitor, 99
Visual Basic
   Account example, 78–82
   pattern compatibility, 77–78
   single-inheritance, 94
Vlissides, John, 28

W

Woolf, Bobby, 134*n*

Also Available from Addison-Wesley

Design Patterns

Elements of Reusable Object-Oriented Software

By Erich Gamma, Richard Helm, Ralph Johnson, and John Vlissides

Addison-Wesley Professional Computing Series

Capturing a wealth of experience about the design of object-oriented software, four top-notch designers present a catalog of simple and succinct solutions to commonly occurring design problems. Previously undocumented, these 23 patterns allow designers to create more flexible, elegant, and ultimately reusable designs without having to rediscover the design solutions themselves.

0-201-63361-2 • Hardcover • 416 pages • ©1995

Pattern Hatching

By John Vlissides

Software Patterns Series

This succinct, example-driven book empowers software developers who are using design patterns, arguably today's most popular object-oriented programming concept. *Design Patterns'* co-author, John Vlissides blends his intimate knowledge of the pattern development process with practical techniques for better pattern application. The result is a thought-provoking guide that will help you improve your next software design by putting patterns to work successfully.

0-201-43293-5 • Paperback • 192 pages • ©1998

Pattern Languages of Program Design 4
By Neil Harrison, Brian Foote, and Hans Rohnert
Software Patterns Series

The fourth volume in a series of books documenting patterns for professional software developers, *Pattern Languages of Program Design 4* represents the current and state-of-the-art practices in the patterns community. The 29 chapters of this book were each presented at recent PLoP conferences and have been explored and enhanced by leading experts in attendance. Representing the best of the conferences, these patterns provide effective, tested, and versatile software design solutions for solving real-world problems in a variety of domains.

0-201-43304-4 • Paperback • 784 pages • ©2000

The Manager Pool
Patterns for Radical Leadership
By Don Olson and Carol Stimmel
Software Patterns Series

As savvy high-tech managers know, the traditional, industrial models of management do not apply to the fluid and dynamic software development environment. Instead, technical management must formulate a more flexible model of management that can grow and change with the technology. The 61 management patterns featured in *The Manager Pool* offer insight into the relationships between developers and their leaders, showing how teams can better work together to develop software. Based on years of experience in the software development trenches, these patterns address many different aspects of technical management, from the dynamic nature of software development, to communicating with the unique programmer personality, to organizing the workspace.

0-201-72583-5 • Paperback • 272 pages • ©2002

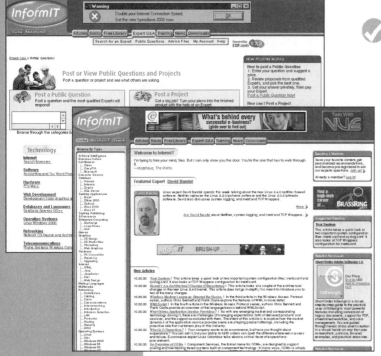